# HOPE REIGNS

How to Conquer Your Mountains Through Courage, Faith, and Perseverance

## DIANNE J. RICHARDSON

Copyright ©2023 Dianne J. Richardson

All rights reserved. No part of this publication may be reproduced, distributed, or transmitted in any form or by any means, including photocopying, recording, or other electronic or mechanical methods, without the prior written permission of the author and publisher, except in the case of brief quotations embodied in reviews and certain other non-commercial uses permitted by copyright law.

Scripture quotations marked (NKJV) are taken from the Holy Bible, New King James Version, Copyright © 1979, 1980, 1982 by Thomas Nelson, Inc. Publishers. Used by permission. All rights reserved.

Scripture quotations are taken from the Holy Bible, New International Version ®, NIV ®, Copyright © 1973, 1978, 1984, 2011 by Biblica Inc.TM. Used by permission of Zondervan. All rights reserved worldwide. www.zondervan.com. The "NIV" and "New International Version" are trademarks registered in the United States Patent and Trademark Office by Biblica, Inc. TM

Scripture quotations marked MSG are taken from The Message by Eugene Peterson. Copyright ©, 1993, 1994, 1995, 1996, 2000, 2001, 2002 used by permission of NavPress Publishing Group. All rights reserved.

Scripture quotations are taken from the Holy Bible, English Standard Version ®, ESV ®, Copyright © 2000, 2001 by Crossway Bibles, a division of Good News Publishers. Used by permission. All rights reserved.

Scripture quotations are taken from the Holy Bible, New Living Translation ®, NLT ®, Copyright © 1996. Used by permission of Tyndale House Publishers, Inc., Wheaton, Illinois 60189. All rights reserved.

Book Cover Design and Interior Formatting by 100 Covers

First Published in 2023

ISBN: 978-1-7384342-0-6

# Dedication

This book is dedicated to my family. I will always love you, even into eternity.

I also dedicate it to you, its reader, in the belief that it may strike a chord with you and give you courage in the darkest of times and hope for a brighter and better future.

My prayer is that God will touch your heart and grant you His, Shalom, Peace.

# Acknowledgements

I would like to thank the following people:

John, my dear husband, who has stood by me, encouraging me every step of my faith, and writing journey, always loved and supported me. God blessed me with the best husband in the world, my steadying captain at the helm.

My daughter Annie, son-in-law Michael - thank you for your love and I give thanks to God for the blessing of my two beautiful granddaughters, Grace, and Hope.

Zana Mwale, for her friendship, constant encouragement and prayers that have helped me through the darkest days, showing me that God's love never fails.

Many pastors and leaders that have taught me through the years:

Martin Holdt, Rev. Sandi Gilfillan, Bobbie Houston, Priscilla Shirer, Christine Caine, Holly Wagner, Joseph Prince, Joyce Meyer, Dr Wendy Treat, Lisa Bevere, Victoria and Joel Osteen, Bishop T.D. Jakes, Brian Houston, Beth Moore, Sheila Walsh, Terry and Jill Eckersley, Sue Sundstrom and Shelli Gardner

And above all, my thankfulness to my God and Father, for helping me to be obedient in following His voice and calling and enabling me to put these words on paper.

# Table of Contents

*Dedication* ............................................................. *iii*

*Acknowledgements* ................................................. *v*

*Introduction* ......................................................... *ix*

GOD SPEAKS – AM I LISTENING? ....................... 1
   1. Hearing the God Whisper ................................. 3
   2. Compassion and Perseverance ........................ 10
   3. Favourite Stories and Purpose ........................ 19
   4. Following the Sound while Wrestling with Grief ... 29
   5. First Greek Trip and a Cave of Hope ............... 40
   6. Colour amid Darkness .................................. 49
   7. Foundations to Rebuild and Restore ............... 62
   8. You are Unique ........................................... 72
   9. You have Unique Purpose ............................. 79

THE STORMS OF LIFE - WEAPONS OF WAR ....... 91
   10. Confronted by Cancer and Death ................... 93
   11. Rhythms of Life .......................................... 113
   12. The Word Anchors ...................................... 121

13. Psalm 23 .................................................. 128
14. Prayer Interludes ...................................... 133

## NEW BEGINNINGS - GOD'S PROMISE ............ 143

15. Setting Sail with Wind in her Sails ............ 145
16. A new Day and a new Era - Forgiven ........ 153
17. Proverbs 31 Woman serves ...................... 158
18. Step out of the Boat ................................. 171
19. Courage, Faith, and Perseverance ............ 184
20. Rainbows and Kisses ................................ 189
21. The Jewel in the Crown ........................... 194
22. The Coronation ....................................... 197
23. A Royal Birth - No other but Jesus .......... 202

*Conclusion* .................................................... 207

*References* .................................................... 215

*About the Author* .......................................... 217

*From the Publisher* ....................................... 219

# Introduction

I heard God say to me: '*You are embarking on a journey that will take you far beyond your natural abilities and capacity, into the realm of faith and the supernatural. Step out beyond your fears and limitations and TRUST me.*' Then He gave me the scripture in John 6:63 (NIV) 'The Spirit gives life; the flesh counts for nothing. The words I have spoken to you, they are full of the Spirit and life.'

Have you ever picked up a book, read the back cover and thought to yourself, I am not ready for this? Could it be that it was hitting a very raw, sensitive area in your life? Do you find yourself in a new struggle, feeling hopeless in your current situation and not being sure where to turn to?

Too many times to be comfortable, I have asked myself the question '*Why did I not learn the lesson sooner and life would have been so much easier.*' and God's reply: '*Dianne, you have been given these mountains to overcome to show others that mountains can be moved.*' I have realised the tests and trials in life take courage and lead us to hope for better outcomes. The struggles we navigate help us develop our faith, conquering our mountains develops perseverance in us and faith leads to our eternal hope.

At times it would seem there is no end to tribulations as they take on what I call, the waterfall effect, cascading one after the other.

I think what I am trying to share with you, is that life never was and never is going to be a walk in the park. How we navigate the storms of life is what counts.

*'When you have come through the valleys and trials, one day you will receive the crown of life. Today is the start of a new season. You will go forth in My strength and with My purposes. I will equip you and uphold you and lead you where you will go. Go in My Name. My Spirit I pour afresh into you, go forth and proclaim Me to your world. Your strength lies in Me and My anointing covers you.'* Selah.

There have been times I have found myself rebelling against God out of sheer frustration, a sense of loss, loneliness, or anger. There have been other seasons when all I wanted to do was put my fingers in my ears and pretend that I had not heard Him. One thing is certain. He never gives up on us. He keeps whispering and when He is not whispering, He nudges.

As you journey with me now, I will share how through times of disillusionment, sorrow, feeling hopeless and even staring death in the face, we can always hold onto hope in the darkest times in life. I want to build you up with encouragement and help you see how I navigated some of these struggles, overcame mountains and walked through valleys, faced death head on, learned so many lessons and how I am still here today doing battle and learning, by the grace of God.

As you face each storm in life and feel like you are drowning, there is an ability to either sit down and give up, or a choice to gather your courage and get up, dust yourself off and persevere. I know this is not a magic formula but there is One far greater than you and I, who gives us the strength and power to overcome if we lean on Him and let Him help us. You may have met Him already and you may not, but I am confident that as I share my story, you will encounter Him along the way.

With each of my challenges, so much has been about deepening my own walk with Jesus and spending dedicated time with Him. I do not think we are ever too old to learn. This, my first book, has been discovering and learning that obedience to God is a non-negotiable.

You are His beloved too and He cares so deeply for you. He never lets us go even when we believe we have lost our way. When He has whispered to you through those quiet moments, He has always been with you and He will never leave your side. He also never gives up on us even if we feel at times like we have given up on Him. He waits patiently in the wings for us. Ultimately, we do not control our own lives even though many of us think that we do. He is the Author of our lives!

For many years I have felt a calling and I have been nudged at various times, to tell my story. Each time, I delayed starting because I often felt that I was not good enough. I have this deep desire to share God's love and did not know how to speak out and gain my voice or to give voice to my thoughts. My first attempt about thirteen years ago, was a blog I felt compelled to write. I was very vulnerable, moved by a verse of scripture that I read following the death of a very close friend, and felt the urgency of getting the words on paper that God was laying on my heart.

Clearly, God knew then that He had so much more to teach me before I would be able to tell my story. I am still learning. I heard Him ask me quietly: '*If it is not you who is going to write it Dianne, then who?*' Friend, may I call you friend? Just as I have been called to write this book, you have not merely stumbled across it. You are reading it because God has a message here for you, so welcome and I feel honoured that you are taking the time to read it, thank you and be blessed.

My prayer is that God will use my story embedded in His story, to bring you hope when everything feels hopeless and when you find those valleys of despair and those chains of bondage engulf you. If you recognise even one small part or some of these battles as your own too, I pray that my sharing with you, will lift you up and encourage you. Show you that He is faithful, and always with you when the road and the battles seem relentless. You are never doing battle on your own. You are never truly alone. He is always by your side. He always provides that lifeline and He will anchor you and keep your head above the water. With Him, you will always come up for air and be able to breathe again to see another day. I pray that you will find courage, hope, strength, and healing as you spend time in His presence. You can prevail over your circumstances. Learning to see life through a lens with an eternity perspective, can change how we navigate the storms of life. We are spiritual people having a human experience and because Jesus is alive today, we have eternal life when we accept Him as our Saviour. To God be all the glory!

I love this quote from Joel Osteen when he says: '*It is time to rise higher. What has limited you in the past does not have to limit you in the future. If you will stay in faith, your story ends in victory.*'

# GOD SPEAKS – AM I LISTENING?

# 1
# Hearing the God Whisper

Mark 16:15 (NIV)
*'He said to them, "Go into all the world and
preach the gospel to all creation.'*

'If you find you are sitting in the gutter one day, there will be one choice that you are faced with. You cannot count on thinking that someone will come along and pick you up or help you out of that gutter. The only person that will make it happen is you. You can choose to stay where you are and the consequences are that you will die, or you can pick yourself up and decide that you can do something to help yourself to live.'

These were the stark words spoken to me by my late father when I was a young teenager growing up. The event that gave rise to this conversation was because I was discouraged and wanting to give up. It was a conversation that seemed incredibly harsh, was meant to teach me a lesson in determination and perseverance, and has remained etched in my mind ever since. I now have a new perspective that I would like to share with you. One of understanding and learning the lesson of never-ending hope, to be courageous in the darkest of times and most traumatic of circumstances. *How is it that there are some conversations that never leave us*, I wonder.

Dad only had one arm when I was born. When I was of an age that I could understand more, I asked him the inevitable question and remember him telling me how he had lost his right arm underground in a mining accident. Although Dad never made a huge thing of the event, there was much more to his story and I would like to share a glimpse with you.

He had been working as an underground operator in the Rhokana Copper mine in Northern Rhodesia, now Zambia. According to the report the Rhokana Corporation published, the accident occurred on the 5th March, 1957 at 11.45am, on the 1850 level, Central Shaft, Nkana. This is how the report written by the officials in charge described that traumatic, dramatic and courageous act that changed multiple lives forever that day.

'*.. A large rock fell from the draw-point onto the centre bar of the grizzley, thence into grizzley crosscut. Kinghorn pushed the Boss Boy aside and in so doing was struck by the rock. Kinghorn and the Boss-boy, who has since resigned, were standing in the crosscut when a large rock fell from the drawpoint above the grizzley and was making its way into the crosscut. As the Boss Boy was standing* *in its line of movement, it can safely be assumed that he would have been crushed to death had it not been for Kinghorn's immediate action in pushing him aside. In the act, however, Kinghorn's outstretched right arm was crushed against the side wall by the rock and had to be amputated.*

*It will be seen from this that Kinghorn's courage and concern for his African co-worker cost him his arm and almost his life. I commend him as a young man of courage...'* signed E.A.B. Phillips, Personnel Manager, for Rhokana Corporation Limited.

If you are unfamiliar with mining terms as I was, the crosscut usually described a level driven across the course of a vein of copper in this case. The grizzly referenced the series of iron or steel bars, spaced to size, sort, or separate the bulk material/rocks as they would fall into the ore chutes. When I read this account only recently of my father's accident, it was a knife twisting in my gut. I could not put myself in that dark underground mining tunnel. Nor could I imagine the pain, fear, and sense of complete helplessness that he must have experienced at the time of the accident. He had been trapped underground for six hours before they were able to bring him to the surface. It showed me that he was someone prepared to sacrifice his life, for the sake of saving his fellow worker. How many people do you know that may be prepared to do the same in today's world?

That traumatic event had taken place a month before my Mum was due to give birth to me. Dad had navigated his way in hospital for the next few months, learning to adapt and live with only one arm, disabled, as well as being thrust into becoming a new father. During this horrendous trauma, my Mum was trying to cope with having given birth to a premature baby, a husband who had nearly lost his life and was now disabled for the rest of his life, and with limited disability income. They both struggled and persevered together.

Years later, when I found myself going through a severe depression, those stark words spoken all those years ago, became the life sustaining words that he had shared. *Where was my courage? Where was the hope I could hold onto?*

It had been tough love at the time (something he became renown for) and a hard conversation and life lesson to absorb. I was determined never to find myself in that gutter. It is a conversation that has been branded forefront and centre in my brain and that suddenly appears from time to time to jolt me back to reality. When I reflect on and try and recall the one thing my father had shared with me during his life, it was this one conversation. Never had I realised the impact this was to have on my life. The moral of that story was to have courage, never give up hope, to have a servant heart and place others before myself and to persevere in all circumstances in life.

Also, no co-incidence then that the school motto of the very first Junior school I attended was '*Persevere*' and the school motto of my Senior High school was '*Facta non Verba – Deeds and not Words.*' Perhaps this explains why I am someone who has always been driven to action in any circumstances and have found it hard, to be quiet and happy with my own company.

To my surprise, I discovered that perseverance is one of the key traits that my brother talks about in his coffee roasting business when he discusses how his journey started. Perhaps it shows how much our childhoods have an impact on our thinking and behaviours. Do you find yourself reflecting on childhood conversations or lessons? How they have helped to shape your life? Sometimes they may not all have been positive or helpful either as has been the case with me. There were many other conversations that were brutally damaging, but now is not the time to explore those.

How fascinating, to unravel these facts and recognise how every step of our lives are already mapped out for us and how God's hand is present and there is purpose in everything. Often, He is communicating with us even when we do not see or hear or do not have an acute awareness of Him. Do we make time to be still and to listen or do we fill our lives with so much busyness that there is never time to listen or time to hear, time to put the puzzle pieces together. Many of us do not think or believe that God can or will speak to us and that it was only the characters in the Bible that He communicated with. Some of us will not believe until we see hard evidence. Others wander around looking for factual evidence before they will believe or step out in faith or into faith. The evangelist and author Charles Stanley once said: *'If we come to Him doubting His ability to speak, we will have a difficult time listening. So, we must come expectantly.'*

I felt guilty at neglecting to place God front and centre and making Him the priority in my life. I know there are times where I become comfortable, far too comfortable. The enemy has power in making us feel guilty because he paralyses us and stops us from doing and achieving all that God has planned and set before us. It is time to take back what he has stolen, time to be alert to the enemy and acting in God's strength, being able to overcome.

In this season, I am hearing the voice of God whispering ever stronger than before and now it is time to put words into action. If I close my eyes, I can see that large image of a white dove with wings spread wide against the backdrop on the screen in the Royal Albert Hall. I am transported back to a Colour Conference in 2009 when Pastor Bobbie Houston, then co-founder of Hillsong Church, had shared her opening teaching about Hearing the Voice of God.

Close your eyes for a moment and picture this in your mind's eye. Imagine you can see the image of a white dove in the top left corner of a large cinema graphic screen, wings spread open wide and flying silently towards the centre. The dove is getting closer and closer and as its wings are moving with a natural but predictable rhythm, the soundless movement at first, becomes louder and louder and even louder still. Then it sounds like a significant wind. With strength and power as the dove is in full flight, you can hear the full motion of the wings moving.

This image of a white dove is still a pictorial representation of the Holy Spirit in many books, stories, and documents. I realise that with the Holy Spirit and with that image comes movement. I know that to be obedient I must be mobilised into action. Obedience to God in this season is about a gear change and no longer sitting back, but stepping forward. It starts with being me and being happy and letting God's light shine in me like the sun on a warm and bright day.

God has created a whole generation of daughters including you and I, for such a time as this. To make this happen I know when clouds of doubt, fear and stress want to stop me from shining, it is about leaning in tighter and pressing into God. He is the Rock and the Light.

I knew in 2009 I was being called to follow that sound. The motion that started out as being very slow and very soothing has grown quicker and louder as the years have passed. Now it is a loud wind thundering in my ears. I can hear the rushing sound of the wings as the dove draws closer and the noise grows louder. God is calling and His voice is calling me.

I have made some poor choices and allowed the busyness of life to be master and get in the way of doing what God has tasked me to do. Fear of failure, fear of exposing some of my innermost thoughts, fear of sharing my guilt and pain, fear of admitting I was wrong or scared – all these are limiting beliefs and lies that the enemy has used to paralyse me. He has bound me in chains time and time again and my struggle for freedom has been so intense at times, that I thought I would sink and drown.

Do you also get faced with thoughts of self-doubt at times and fear of failure and what have they stopped you from doing or achieving that may have been very important to you?

I have questioned whether my experiences and insights are even relevant or impactful enough to make a difference in someone else's life. Then I hear Him saying that this story is meant for the 'one' and He knows the 'one.'

# 2
# Compassion and Perseverance

By way of an interlude, I must deviate and share another's story. Have you heard of the organisation called Compassion? Compassion is a leading Christian children's charity. Today, 'Compassion partners with more than 8,000 churches in 25 countries to deliver their proven child development programme to more than 2 million infants, children, and youth. Around the world, children, families, and entire communities are being empowered to overcome poverty and thrive both now and into the future.'[1] Compassion website: https://www.compassionuk.org/about-us/who-we-are/. Their programme works through a project of sponsorship.

Compassion. Have you ever stopped to think carefully about the true meaning of the word compassion? My father and my grandfather before him, were men I always thought of as having compassionate hearts. They would demonstrate this at different times when confronted with anyone in need. Then there is the greatest example of all, Jesus. His life was a life of compassion sacrificed for you and I.

I was first introduced to the Charitable organisation Compassion, at a Conference when Pastor Gary Clarke, former Senior Pastor at Hillsong London, gave a talk about the programme and what its aims are. He had set the scene and encouraged us to prayerfully consider sponsoring a child through this initiative. The summarising point he shared which touched a very deep chord within me, was that if every one person was prepared to sponsor even one child, with the number of ladies that were in the audience at the conference on that day, we would be able to sponsor a whole village together. That was the moment I recognised that I really could make a difference by reaching that 'one' child through the sponsorship initiative and that as an individual, I could make a real difference in someone else's life.

Have you ever felt like you do not have a voice of your own or that you are too small on your own to make a difference? Have you felt the urge to speak out about something you feel strongly convicted about and found that when you open your mouth to speak, words have failed you? What action have you taken or has it rendered you unable to act? Have you found yourself feeling bound, with both hands tied behind your back?

Through all these past years of trials and mountains to scale and valleys to navigate, I have had to learn to trust God, to place my trust fully in Him. As a believer in the Word of God, I know with absolute certainty that there is the one book in history that will always exist and that its teachings and truths are real, namely *The Bible*. How do I know this? It is very explicitly shown to us in Isaiah 40:8 [NIV] *'The grass withers and the flowers fall, but the word of our God endures forever.'* I have grown in learning that it is by His Word that He has given me strength and hope. I have realised afresh that it is never too late to answer His call and listen to His voice. This quote from one of the Colour conference invitations summed it all up very succinctly: *'The greatest story ever told is that of God's Son, who came from Heaven to earth to secure our freedom. The Bible says that He returned to heaven to prepare for our homecoming.'*[2] Brochure 2010 conference. I know that all these past experiences in my life have been etched with God's signature as a way of preparing me for the next stage of this journey.

What are the life experiences you have been through or struggles that you may still be attempting to navigate? I am sure there are some that will be very similar to what I am going to share. Did you find yourself wanting someone to talk to through some of these stages of those experiences and yet finding it was hard to identify someone that could relate to what you were going through? Perhaps you felt isolated and very alone, possibly filled with fear of the unknown and what was still to unfold before you. Were you offered counselling through any of those really difficult times and how did you feel about engaging with a counsellor?

Not everyone has the strength or sometimes the courage to acknowledge that they need counselling for fear that it may make them look like a failure or communicate to others that maybe they do not have faith or that their faith is not strong enough. I found it becomes a vicious circle because it leaves you feeling even more of a failure. I felt too scared to step out and ask for that help that I knew I so desperately wanted. These are all thoughts that I have wrestled with at various low points. Yes, finally following a nervous breakdown years ago when it all became too much to cope with, I did seek counselling. As much as I was always the first person to pooh-pooh getting help, I am now the biggest advocate of recommending working with a counsellor. This does not negate my faith either.

It was before Covid that God highlighted this verse of scripture to me in Isaiah 41:10 (NLT) *'Don't be afraid, for I am with you. Do not be discouraged, for I am your God. I will strengthen you and help you. I will hold you up with my victorious right hand.'* Some people or even bible scholars may contest this and say *'How do you know God was saying this to you or meant it for you? The Bible was written in a different time and with a different purpose and context?'* and to them I reply God has said that His word is written for everyone and that He will reveal Himself to all who earnestly seek Him. I believe the Bible is God's breathed words meant for all who will have ears to hear Him speak through it to us. It is not exclusive and excludes no-one. Psalm 66:16 [NLT] *'Come and listen, all you who fear God, and I will tell you what he did for me.'* I know now that my story matters and that I must not be afraid to tell it. I also know that the title for this book is one that He has directed and blessed me with. It is derived from Isaiah 40:9 (NIV) *'You who bring good news to Zion, go up on a high mountain. You who bring good news to Jerusalem, lift up your voice with a shout, lift it up, do not be afraid; say to the towns of*

*Judah, here is your God!*' Shortly after this, Covid hit the world and we all found ourselves amid the pandemic. I held onto God's promise in Isaiah 41 to not fear.

In parallel and as though I was a looking at a bright neon sign, I saw the word Perseverance in my mind. James 1:4 (NIV) 'Let perseverance finish its work so that you may be mature and complete, not lacking anything.' And through my life lessons, this translates as:

P = PATIENCE – being patient in every situation

E = EAGER – being eager to listen and do God's work daily

R = READY – ready for battle

S = STEADFAST – believing in His promises, filled with hope, never giving up

E = ETERNAL – the life that awaits with Him in eternity that He is preparing me for

V = VOICE – of God, hearing His voice and listening to Him; finding my own voice in His

E = EAR – to be quiet and listen to Him as He speaks in a quiet whisper

R = RIGHTEOUS = remaining in Him, keeping His ways. I am made righteous through Jesus

A = ALERT – to the prowling enemy, and acting in God's strength to overcome adversity

N = NEW = a new creation, a new life promised in Christ Jesus forever

C = CHRIST-like – following His example and living in His ways, cleansed forever

E = ENCOURAGE – to build others up and help strengthen, showing them there is eternal hope and telling them to have courage to face tomorrow

## EVEN APOSTLES STRUGGLED

When I studied more about the life that the Apostle Paul led, why was I not surprised to discover that it was not an easy one. In 2 Corinthians chapter 11 and vs 16 -29 we are told of all his difficulties in life. He tells us how he struggled. He was imprisoned, beaten, stoned and shipwrecked, had gone hungry on multiple occasions and faced death multiple times. Paul describes it this way in 2 Corinthians 4:8-9 (NIV): '*We are hard-pressed on every side, yet not crushed; we are perplexed, but not in despair; persecuted, but not forsaken; struck down, but not destroyed.*' Many of these struggles were way beyond anything that I have experienced or could even imagine. Yet, through all these trials God was there and through all his challenges, Paul clung to the hope of the Word of God and the promises of God. '*Therefore, we do not lose heart. Though outwardly we are wasting away, yet inwardly we are being renewed day by day. For our light and momentary troubles are achieving for us an eternal glory that far outweighs them all. So, we fix our eyes not on what is seen, but on what is unseen, since what is seen is temporary, but what is unseen is eternal.'* 2 Corinthians 4:16-18 (NIV).

We know and are told in the Bible that in this world we will have trouble but they also prove that our faith is real. We are told in James chapter 1:2-3 (NIV) *'consider it pure joy... whenever you face trials of many kinds because you know that the testing of your faith produces perseverance...'*

Paul is not ashamed of the gospel and his primary aim was to share the love of Jesus and the promise of what was to come in our eternal hope and life, with others. When we can see the eternal rather than the temporary, we can share it with others and we can do this through sharing about our lives and our stories and by using our creative gifts. This mobilises me to be living and leaning on His promises for my life, daily. I have the certainty and assurance of that from Joshua 1:9: (NLT) 'This is my command - *Be strong and courageous. Do not be afraid or discouraged. For the Lord your God is with you wherever you go."* I know with certainty that He has my back covered. He has gone before me; He goes behind me and shields and protects me.

At my first Colour Conference attendance, I recall Pastor Bobbie Houston spoke of hearing the voice of God being a Whisper. *'One word from God can change your life forever!'* I thought back to that one piece of information that my earthly father had shared with me all those years back about perseverance and how that had a profound impact on my life. How much greater was the impact of what my Heavenly Father was telling me. Still, shockingly, I chose to put aside what He was telling me once that conference was over.

For the years that followed there have been a myriad of God nudges. Those God whispers have not let up. I have been taught so many lessons through the times of struggles, in climbing the mountains that have risen before me and then finding myself in the dark and treacherous valleys. I will attempt to share some of these with you and what has enabled me to scale them and finally reach the summit of one mountain, before being thrown into an abyss and again finding myself in the valleys and depths and having my next mountain ahead of me to climb. I have been learning through these experiences that when we learn we can put our weaknesses before Jesus, God's transforming power comes through and we find a God given strength to bring us through as we persevere. James 1:3 (NIV) *'let perseverance finish its work so that you may be mature and complete, not lacking anything.'*

Isaiah 43:19: (NLT) *'For I am about to do something new. See, I have already begun! Do you not see it? I will make a pathway through the wilderness. I will create rivers in the dry wasteland.'* Time for me to set aside all the vulnerabilities and concerns about exposing the 'raw' me and to be me. My totally imperfect and authentic self. I realised that my wounds can become the source of my greatest strengths. When I have tried to manage my pain and despair in the past by always burying myself in so much busyness and work, I have used it as a coping mechanism and an excuse. I know that the lives He is touching now and wants me to share the gospel with, is what really matters. God has taught me that His agenda is about getting the gospel and the message of Jesus into this broken world I live in. Jesus is a cause worth living and dying for.

But, I want to set the record straight. This story was never going to be only about me. It is His story that has been planted in my heart. I am an ongoing imperfect work of His. I would not have come this far or even be here now, if it was not for God's incredible love for me and He has that same unconditional and generous love for you. When we decide to give our lives to Him, we do not do anything on our own anymore and He writes the pages of our stories.

I have a quiet confidence now is the time for this story because He has promised to watch over me in this. *'I will instruct you and teach you in the way you should go; I will guide you with My eye.'* [NKJV] This verse in Psalm 32:8 was shown to me as I started my writing. If we can change the way we look at life we will soon see that each blessing that God gives us will be a reason to be a blessing to someone else.

# 3
# Favourite Stories and Purpose

Story, so what does the word story mean? There are multiple definitions for the word *story*. It can be defined as a narrative; other definitions describe it as a tale or an account of a journey travelled, facts or experiences that deserve narration. One of the definitions in the Cambridge Dictionary is that a story can be a description, either true or imagined, of a connected series of events. As I embark on this story, I will be relaying true events that have occurred in my life. I may not always be entirely accurate when it comes to describing places and I ask for your understanding in this regard.

Coming back to the word *Story*. When you think of a story, what was one of your most favourite stories you can remember growing up as a child? Was it an adventure? Perhaps it was fantasy of a damsel in distress being rescued by her knight in shining armour? Was it a mystery or could it have been a very scary story that made such a deep impression on you as a child, that you can even feel the chills go up and down your spine if you think of it today? I should imagine depending on the generation you were born into; it is going to vary and probably be about how far back you can remember into your childhood. Some psychologists that have studied Child Developmental Psychology would say that our earliest memories that we generally recall are from about the age of 3 or sometimes 4 years old. If you think back to your earliest childhood memories, can you remember how old you were? It makes for an interesting exercise.

Almost daily we are exposed to part of people's stories or we even become a part of someone else's story. I was given fresh inspiration by a new story that I heard not so long ago. The person in question is fondly known by the British public as "thefridgeman." Michael Copeland is a former soldier and he was being interviewed on the BBC Breakfast program as he completed the Three Peaks challenge by carrying a fridge on his back. He had decided to climb the highest mountains in England, Scotland and Wales for this challenge and has raised thousands of pounds for the mental health charity, Mind. He explained that the fridge represented the heavy burden of carrying around mental health issues and negative thoughts. He told how having struggled with mental health issues related to a lot of negative thoughts, he realised that physical activity and nature had become a positive outlet to manage stress and an outlet for negative issues. He had set about walking and climbing mountains to raise awareness for mental health and the charity Mind. Did you know that according to Mind, around one out of every four people in the U.K. struggle with a mental health problem each year?

It was what he shared at the conclusion of his interview that resonated with me, that our mental health is on us, you, and I. Each of us must look after own mental health. Here was a former soldier who has experienced mountains he has had to climb in his life, both figuratively and literally and that is so typical of so many of us. The fridge strapped to his back is representative of all the troubles, worries and challenges that we face and they become burdens. His summary in saying that we are responsible for our own mental health hit the nail on the head, however, we have a choice. We can try and do that on our own or we can look to someone far greater than us to carry the burden for us.

## SHADOW THE SHEEPDOG

So now, let me get back to my favourite book that I read as a child. For me, it is the Enid Blyton book called *Shadow the Sheepdog*. I was an avid Enid Blyton addict as she was the first author that truly inspired me to develop a love of and a joy in reading.

I love animals, farming, and nature and especially dogs, so it was inevitable that this tale of *Shadow the sheepdog* and his master Johnny was going to capture my imagination. I was desperate to have a dog of my own and this catapulted me into Johnny's world. He longed for a dog of his own too. His father was a farmer and owned Jessie. Jessie gave birth to a litter of three pups and whilst they were all sold, one kept returning to the farm. Finally, his father relented and Johnny was allowed to keep the mischievous pup that was to be called Shadow. Shadow never left his side and although much was to be learned from the other dogs on the farm, Johnny trained the puppy himself. What Johnny did not realise was that Shadow was also teaching him a few very important and valuable lessons about life. Why does that not sound unfamiliar?

You cannot put a price on the love that a dog gives you so unconditionally. What does unconditional love trigger in your mind? Surely there is only One who can love us totally unconditionally given all our flaws and failures. He is always in the shadow. Then there's Johnny's experience of taking the sheep and some lambs to market one day. He forgets to count the lambs as he is distracted by his lunch. He is forced to confess to his father later that he had forgotten to count the lambs and had only been saved because of Shadow's vigilance in going back and retrieving the missing lamb. A key innocent lesson in honesty. One that was still praiseworthy. His father recognised the brave honesty of his son in owning up to the mistake of having left a lamb behind. Would every child be this honest?

This childhood favourite story reminded of the parable in Matthew 18:10 – 14, when Jesus goes back for the one lamb that was lost. It demonstrates that you cannot depend on many things in this world but there is one thing we can count on with certainty and that is that God's Word will always be true and the promises in His Word will never fail. Nothing can separate us from the unconditional love of God. (Isaiah 61:1-3) He cares for us all equally and He will stop everything else to find and care for us if we will let Him. Jesus went back to find the one lost sheep and He will find anyone who is lost.

I am so privileged to be a child of God and to know that I am part of His greatest love story. The one about how He sent His one and only Son, Jesus Christ, to come into this world and then to be crucified and die for you and me so that we may have everlasting life beyond the grave. I feel like I was once that lost lamb that Jesus came back for. If you may be lost, He will come back for you too. God will never leave us (Romans 8:39). He is always in the shadow.

God has kept calling and calling and calling and now I cannot deny His power. It has led me to a place of humble longing to share His incredible love with you and to help you hear His voice calling you too.

## HAVE YOU FOUND YOUR PURPOSE?

Have you found your purpose in life or do you know what it is? I grappled with this question for years. Now, as a Christian communicator I want to share Christ's story and how His story has made a way for my story and He wants to be a part of your story too. Perhaps as you are reading this you can identify strongly with what I am sharing. Perhaps it sounds quite alien to you. If it is the latter, I know that it is not an accident that you are now reading about Him and His love for you in some of these pages.

One small whisper from God can shake mountains. If you ask me how this is possible, I will say to you that it takes courage to dig deep. Sometimes you must dig even deeper than you thought was possible and through His strength which is made perfect in our weaknesses, with Jesus carrying the burden, we can survive. With only a small whisper from God, the mountains shake. When God speaks, it is in His perfect timing and to accomplish His agenda not our own. If we do not want to wait sometimes for God's timing but try and drive forward with our own agenda and timelines, we can harm ourselves more by causing major disasters or problems because we do not see the full picture or know the whole context. Only God knows and sees all and we need to wait for directions according to the right time that only God knows. Jesus taught this lesson to his disciples when He said in John 16:12 (NLT): *'There is so much more I want to tell you, but you cannot bear it now.'*

Fast forward to a Sunday morning a few months ago. I was listening to Pastor Joseph Price giving his Sunday teaching at New Creation Church in Singapore. Got you. Although I may have wished I was seated in that gathering in Singapore, I was not there in person. I was watching and listening to the broadcast service online. How awesome that we can do that with modern technology. We can traverse time and space to participate in worship even when it happens across the globe from where we are. Pastor Prince was telling us to *'rise up and get our voices out there'* and *'to write our message down.'* Another God whisper? I found myself faced with a choice. The question I needed to answer *'was I going to be obedient this time or was I going to let this opportunity slip by again?'*

Have you ever read the book *The Pilgrim's Progress by John Bunyan*? It is primarily a story written with lots of symbolism that describes a good man's pilgrimage in life. It tells of all the challenges, despair, and trials, but how he is sustained through his Christian journey until he reaches the '*celestial city.*' What a strange question to be asking you may say. This book, has real significance in this story because it is the book I was gifted on the day I went through adult baptism, at fourteen years old. Little did I know then, that this book that spoke of Pilgrim's journey would be a reflection in part of my own life's journey.

To date my life has been what has felt like a pilgrimage, one step at a time. There have been many hardships, challenges, illness, trials, pain, and death along the way. These have been counter-balanced by times of great joy, laughter, celebration, and survival. The scene around me has constantly changed. I have lived and worked in multiple countries across the globe experiencing multicultural societies, learning so much from all of them. When someone recently asked me what my nationality is, I replied '*I am a citizen of heaven and on earth I am a global citiz*en.'

It was only when I was hospitalised multiple times this year, that I felt this great sense of urgency and heard God telling me that it was no longer an option to delay telling this story. The story of how much our Heavenly Father loves you and I, why He will always be our eternal Hope, especially when life gets tough and throws mountains in our path.

Perhaps it was because I felt the fragility of life again and realised that each breath that I take is because God is breathing that life into me. My heart skipped a beat and instead of feeling low and downcast as I was when I had been admitted to hospital, I now felt invigorated as a realised my new sense of purpose.

From a life under threat and attack, to a life where blood is flowing through my veins and that is flourishing. I recognise how each part of our journeys are interwoven and none of the experiences that we go through along the way are without purpose. Whether these be good or bad, God uses every situation that we have been put in and gone through, for good.

I have mentioned my two little granddaughters. I firmly believe that it is God given insight and blessing that led our daughter and son-in-law to name them Grace and Hope respectively. There is a full story woven into each of their names and I count myself as truly blessed that God has shown His love to me in yet such another incredible and profound way. The abundant blessing of these two beautiful girls is beyond description.

I find myself welling up, swallowing hard and quite emotional, as I stop to take it all in. There is not a day that passes when I do not get reminded that I have both Grace and Hope in my life, two of the greatest promises of God for us.

## THE MODERN DAY 'WOMEN OF GOD'

I want to pause for a moment and reflect some of the modern day *'women of God'* - a whole army of them if you take a moment to stop and look around you. Everyone seems so together and to have it all together. They all appear to be successful and to be achieving what I saw myself wanting to do. My life has been full and there have been many achievements along the way, but these recognitions have left me with a sense that there is still so much more to do. This is not about personal achievement for my own benefit, but it is about achieving what God wants us, all His daughters to accomplish, for the purposes of building His Kingdom and supporting each other in the process.

In many of the messages that modern-day women of God share, they bring the women of the past that have gone before, to the fore. Great women in the Bible like Mary, Elizabeth, Esther, Ruth, Rahab, Delilah, Lydia. This is not the exhaustive list. *Which of these would I identify with most* I asked myself and if you were to ask this question of yourself too, what would your answer be? Who do you see as having similar traits or behaviours or belief systems to those you have? Is it an easy question to answer? Do you know who they are?

It was time to stop and ask: '*Where do I start God and how do I do this?*' A big lesson for me is that as I have been writing, I have been spending more time in His Word and in part I have still been healing. I have discovered that God has a way of re-directing my priorities. He has been bringing me healing in some very tender and raw, wounded areas in my life. If we want God to show up, we must be prepared to create that place and a space for Him to show up. His timeline is also never our timeline and the way that we want to rush things and make them happen of our own free will is not always going to achieve the outcomes that we are looking for.

He has been teaching me too, that not only is my story meant to be an instrument that He will use, but it has been about teaching me how important it is that I spend more time studying His Word. I must let go of control and realise that it is not about me thinking I am going to fill the pages in the book. I must learn to leave the pages blank and allow Him to guide me in what will be important to share. I am learning that it is about being guided, more fully present with Him and allowing Him to lead.

All scripture is God breathed. There are still so many more messages to discover and lessons to be learned. This is only the beginning of my new purpose and I am excited, truly excited for what He is still revealing. I know that this book is my purpose for Him and letting go and daring to do what He has called me to do. Are there areas in your life where you are always in control? It is not an easy process and perhaps like me, to discover your real purpose, you need to let go of control?

# 4
# Following the Sound while Wrestling with Grief

Silence! The beautiful, bright cerise pink bougainvillaea was even more striking against the backdrop of the turquoise and ink blue sea. It contrasted starkly against the brilliant whitewashed walls and blue domes of the Grecian clifftops of Oia on Santorini. Oia is a coastal town on the north western tip of Santorini and this island is an absolute jewel in the crown of the Greek Pellagos. I was fascinated with the cave houses dug into the volcanic rock of the rugged clifftops. As I stood and gazed across to the horizon, I was overlooking the vast caldera, with signs of whispers of steam along a ridge of rocky outcrop in the bay. Yes, the volcano is still active.

Generally, the white, rusty orange and purple bougainvillea, are the most prominent ones in the species. I had to reach out and touch the paper-like blossoms. They were so delicate and almost square in their shape and interestingly, they were tissue thin to the touch. I was surprised to discover their beguiling beauty did not include a fragrance that I was aware of.

If you have visited one of the beautiful Greek islands and possibly even Santorini, I am sure you can feel the fresh sea breeze on your skin now if you close your eyes and as you drink in the beauty around you. Feel the brilliant hot sun baking the skin on your arms. Did you know that Santorini is also a natural wonder of the world because of its famous volcano that was formed because of a massive volcanic eruption, thousands of years ago. The day I stepped onto the Santorini soil, the air was so fresh and yet pregnant with the aroma of the atmosphere that picture postcards are made of, and heavy with thyme, oregano, and citrus notes. I now understood why it is best known for its breath-taking sunsets.

I was still in deep reflection after disembarking from the ship that had I cruised on from Crete. I felt tired as it had been a very early start. I had to be in Heraklion at 4.30am to make sure I boarded in time for our departure that day. The first sight that drew my attention as we approached our destination port, were the famous blue domes of Santorini. They are famous world over. I think almost every poster, travel brochure or postcard of Santorini has these as their main image. They must be the most photographed domes of the Greek islands. These blue domes are in Oia on Santorini and are the cliff edge churches of Saint Spyridon and the Church of the Resurrection.

## HOLY SPIRIT VISION AND HOPE

In my mind's eye I had the vision of that beautiful white dove on the large screen as captured me again. All I could hear was the sound of its wings swooping up and down as it was in full flight and sweeping towards me. If you are one of the thousands of beautiful daughters that have ever been to a Hillsong Colour Women's conference, you may even have seen this image or possibly even shared the experience with me if you attended the same conference. It was mesmerising. At that moment, I knew that the dove, representing the Holy Spirit, was beckoning me, calling me – and I knew I had to follow the sound.

You may be asking how I know that the white dove symbolises the Holy Spirit. If we read the following passages in the Bible, when Jesus was baptised, we see the Holy Spirit referenced as a dove. The heavens opened and the Holy Spirit descended upon him in the form of a dove. Matthew 3:16 (NIV) *'as soon as Jesus was baptized, he went up out of the water. At that moment heaven was opened, and he saw the Spirit of God descending like a dove and alighting on him;'* and in Mark 1:10 NIV) *'Just as Jesus was coming up out of the water, he saw heaven being torn open and the Spirit descending on him like a dove'* and in Luke 3:22 (NIV) *'and the Holy Spirit descended on him in bodily form like a dove. And a voice came from heaven: You are my Son, whom I love; with you I am well pleased;'* and in John 1:32 (NIV) *'Then John gave this testimony: I saw the Spirit come down from heaven as a dove and remain on him.'*

The event speakers were all lined up for the next three days and I was eager to hear the messages they would be sharing with us. I knew in my spirit that this was going to be an experience like no other. God had touched my spirit in those opening moments and I felt highly sensitised. This could mean only one thing and I instinctively knew it meant God was going to do business with me and I was alert and listening. My wounds were raw. I was in the deep and darkest pit of pain. All I knew was the deep aching in my chest that could not be shifted was like no other trauma or illness I had experienced before.

If you have lost a loved one through death, you will understand the deep, raw emotions that engulf you. Or how has it affected you? Did you acknowledge that you were grieving? Are you still in a stage of grief? Psychologists say that it is a process and they will describe either five or seven stages of grief. You go through shock, denial, anger, bargaining, depression and then acceptance and hope and processing your grief. My experience is that I do not think grief ever leaves you. I think it takes on a different form and a different meaning over time. I have also experienced grief very differently in the case of the deaths of both my parents and when my mother-in-law died. One theory is that the grief that remains is representative of love. But I think grief made me realise that even when someone you love dies, there is hope. We have hope in knowing that we will be reunited with them one day in God's eternal kingdom. Death is not the end.

Death is a journey. It is a raw experience and grief is a unique process, separate to dying and death. Some people process death immediately and if you are like me, it has taken me years to process grief. *Does grief ever get to feel less painful or easier to cope with? Do you ever really accept death of someone you loved very deeply?* If you have experienced death of a loved one or a friend, how have you processed and experienced it and can you identify with any or all these stages? Are you possibly still working through one of these stages and trying to cope or make sense of your loss? Especially if it is the first death that you experience or if that loss is of your first parent or a child of yours or a spouse, a partner perhaps.

I give thanks to God that we have not experienced the loss of a child, although we came close, but I know some of you will have been through this. In our current decade there are also a great number of parents who have lost children to suicide, which has been on the increase particularly in the under 35 age group. Death is very real and a part of all our daily lives.

Allow me to share with you people who are making a difference and whose courage have really touched and spoken to my heart. There are two groups that have been on walking campaigns to raise awareness of suicide in honour of the children they lost, and raise funds for their respective charities in the U.K. I want to introduce you to their invaluable and heart rendering initiatives.

'*Suicide is the biggest killer of those under 35 in the UK. We only learned this terrifying fact because our daughters took their own lives within the last 3 years. By raising awareness, we hope we can help prevent other families from being devastated by suicide.*' https://www.3dadswalking.uk/[3].

The three Dads, namely, Mike, Andy and Tim undertook and completed their walk successfully in 2022 for their daughters Beth, Sophie, and Emily.

'*We want to continue to highlight the fact that suicide is the biggest killer of young people across the entire UK. We realise that wherever you live in the UK, suicide is a tragic part of so many people's lives. By walking between the parliaments of the 4 nations we will highlight the help PAPYRUS can offer across the UK.*' https://www.3dadswalking.uk/[4].

And in the past few weeks, the second group, this time three Mums, have undertaken a similar initiative walking 200 miles and successfully completing it. Here is where you will find a little about each of the stories of Michelle – Maxi's Mum, Kim – Haden's Mum and Liz – Seb's Mum. It is their headline that drew my attention, specifically because it centres on '*Hope*' and this is what it is '*Just 3 Mums Walking and Raising Awareness, One Step of HOPE at a Time.*'

'*On average, over five young people take their lives each day and over 200 schoolchildren are lost to suicide every year.*

*We only learned of this terrifying fact because our young sons took their lives, all within the last 3 years. Our loss and shock is all encompassing but, with the support of PAPYRUS, we are raising awareness by walking over 200 miles for all those young people as well as our boys, who are lost every year. Our aim is to help prevent other families from being devastated by suicide, particularly as research shows that with appropriate early intervention and support like that offered by PAPYRUS, suicide by young people can be prevented.*

*Our walk is about HOPE, something that is key to what we want to achieve for our boys and for other young people'* https://www.justthreemums.org.uk/[5]

Have you stopped to consider your own mortality because I think that is what a death does. It puts us in a position to ask the questions and the biggest one of all. What happens when I die? There are many who do not ever want to talk about death and treat it as a totally taboo subject. *But, we all have HOPE.*

Initially I had built this wall of steel around me whilst trying to process my grief. I did not want anyone to see or know what I was feeling. In part, I felt like I was not allowed to show my emotions or my grief. My grief was private and in the early stages of my loss following the initial shock, I was angry. Angry at my father for dying, angry at the world around me that seemed to carry on as normal as though nothing had changed, and angry at God, for allowing my father to die before I had time to reconcile my broken relationship with him. In an odd way I was angry at myself and felt responsible and guilty that I had not succeeded in getting my parents to reconcile their broken relationship in prior years. This had led to their divorce eventually and a breakdown of relationships.

# RELATIONSHIPS ARE HARD

Relationships are hard and they need a lot of nurturing, work and communication and sharing. When my parent's marriage fell apart, a part of my world also disintegrated and imploded. Although I tried to urge communication between my father and my mother, I felt guilty that I was relieved when they separated. There was a part of me that believed this was the best outcome for everyone because of my father's infidelity and I held so much anger towards him. This was not how my life was meant to be turning out and I kept asking myself where God was in all of this. It was another stage of growth and learning where I now recognise that God was my strength through all that time and how He carried me, especially on the days that I did not want to carry on and do this anymore. Life had become too hard. The lesson for me was when we are weak, that is when God is able. He is also able to do far more than we can ever hope for or even begin to imagine.

The trauma of my father's recent death back then, was still vivid in my mind and I was still raw with emotion and in shock, numb to the world. I could not tell you which part of the process or which stage of that journey I was at on that day in Santorini. On the cruise it had felt like I was living the moment all over again, like a ground hog day.

The phone's shrill ringing cut through the air. We had walked through the front door. My husband was closest to the phone. '*Hello*' I heard him say as I wandered into the kitchen and left him in the hallway. A few seconds later he was standing in front of me. '*She is here next to me now. Just a moment and I will pass the phone to her.'* He looked at me, his face was expressionless and I felt my heart skip a beat. *What was going on? Who was involved?* These were the immediate questions racing through my mind.

My brother lives in South Africa and I live in the U.K. and we rarely spoke on the phone back then as overseas telephone calls were expensive. I took the phone from my husband and then the stark words were ringing in my ears. *'It is your brother. He wants to talk to you.'* he said as he handed me the phone. Unusually, he did not move away and stood right in front of me. I took the handset and cheerily said *'Hello John. This is a lovely surprise! How are you?'* The bomb dropped soon after. I dropped the handset. *'Dianne, I am so sorry. I am so sorry. I have got very bad news. Dad died earlier this afternoon. He had a massive heart attack and he is dead! We think it was at about 1.30pm this afternoon. Stella had gone out to the shops and when she returned, she found him lying on the bathroom floor. He was dead.'*

As I reeled from the shock of this message that my brother had communicated to me, I dropped the telephone as my legs suddenly felt weak underneath me and I found it too difficult to stand. Ringing in my ears I heard a shrill *'Noooooooo, Oh noooooo!'* as I collapsed in a heap, moaning in the deepest pain I had ever felt in my life. Then as quickly as I had started sobbing, I fought back the tears and steeled up.

The rest of that weekend remains a complete blur even to this day. I only recall crying and walking around and repeating over and over to myself and to my husband. *'Dad's dead, Dad's died. This cannot be happening. Why did God allow this to happen? I had not spoken to him for such a long time. It is my fault. I should have phoned him last Sunday to wish him a Happy Father's Day.'* A phone call I never made and a last conversation I never had would haunt me for days, weeks and years to come.

Do you have memories that haunt you? Have you ever found yourself in a damaged and broken relationship? Has it been once or possibly even several times? Have you wondered how you could ever be restored again to fullness and wholeness and imagined that the damage has been so intense that it is beyond coming back from?

Relentless, that is what pain can feel like sometimes. Are there times in your life when you have felt the onslaughts are too much to bear because they simply do not stop and with each one you feel like you are being pounded further and further into the ground? Have you found yourself living with deep regrets because of broken and damaged relationships? Perhaps you have been feeling the pain of a recent broken relationship or the deepest pain of losing a love of your life?

I had a broken relationship with my father for years and when I lost him, I had not been able to reconcile that relationship with him before he died. I had hurt and I had been hurt and I had totally avoided the whole area of being reconciled with him. Through my lens of pain and pride I had not been able to bring myself to a place to see his perspective. I suspect with him it was also his pride that had got in the way.

Now, years later God was teaching me an old lesson. I was being taught that two wrongs never make a right. This is also a phrase my youngest little granddaughter quoted at her sister one day whilst we were visiting. Wisdom and truth also out of the mouth of babes. The saddest part of all is that I would never be given the opportunity now to ever set that right with my earthly father again.

# 5
# First Greek Trip and a Cave of Hope

Near the village of Spilia on the island of Crete which lies about 25 km west of the town of Chania and 3 km from Kolymbari, you will find the famous historical cave of Saint John. (I knew discovering this cave was no coincidence and another step in God's plan for me. My father's name was John.) It is believed that this saint of Crete founded the simple and frugal tradition of the island. Slowly, I followed the small group I had joined for this excursion as we climbed the stone steps that wound their way up against the hillside. Then it appeared before us, the small cave with a temple from the 15th century. It is still a tradition that on Christmas eve a small nativity play is staged here.

As I stood in that small cave church, the Cave Church of Agios Ioannis (or St. John), a tiny haven of peace on the island of Crete, a week after my father had died, I was still in shock, numb with pain but looking for comfort. As I drank in the humble structure of this tiny place of worship, I noticed where there were a few icons on display and what appeared to be a bronze lampstand with an ornately designed rim that resembled lace. It held several burning candles that cast a soft light and a few shadows against the dark interior of the cave.

I know the catholic church has a practice of lighting a candle in memory of a loved one but it was not a practice I was familiar with or had practiced before. I stood silently and then moved forward tentatively, as I reached for a candle and put my coins into the moneybox beside the candles. I lit a candle and said my first prayer for my father. This was my first acknowledgement that he was no longer with us. That soft and warm light emitted by the candle represented the hope for me in knowing that my father was now clothed in light, an eternal light. As I had stood at his open grave the week before, I had a vision of a golden chalice being taken up a golden flight of stairs, stairs that led into the heavens. The light was so bright I could not look into it and all I could focus on was the golden stairs and the peace that I was clothed with in those fleeting moments.

Sometimes I think this is the hardest part. Being able to acknowledge that the person you have loved and lost are now no longer here. I hoped that my action of lighting a candle in his memory and praying and asking for forgiveness, would set the record straight for me and that I would be able to move on. I knew that my father's physical body was no longer here on earth and that his spirit lives on. I was expecting to feel like suddenly everything would start feeling a bit lighter and easier to cope with. Instead, I was left with the huge emptiness, a void that would last forever and all the guilt that I would carry because of this broken relationship and rejection for years to come.

My grief and loss came in waves in the following years. The first time that the grief tsunami drowned me, was as the Christmas season approached six months after my father had died. At the time of his death and during the whole period of the funeral arrangements and at his actual burial, I was unable to cry. Does that shock you? I had steeled myself and held my emotions in a vice. I knew that I had to be strong for both my mother and my brother. Although we had all experienced grief and loss before when my grandparents had died, this was different for all of us. Mum was losing the love of her life (and even though they had been divorced many years previously, I knew in my heart that Dad was still the true love of her life) and my brother was losing his anchor in life. As the older sibling, I had to keep myself together and be there to support both him and Mum the best way I knew how.

No-one had prepared me for this and there was no way of knowing what I was supposed to do. At that point in time to me that meant no tears, or weeping under any circumstances and keeping my emotions tightly bound and locked up. I had grown quite well accomplished at concealing my emotions because of not being allowed to cry as a child growing up. Does this perhaps strike a chord with you, I wonder?

Six months later, with a heavy work schedule and family responsibilities needing attention, I found myself with only weeks to prepare for Christmas. It had become a practice for us as a family, to host a group of friends and guests on Christmas day. They ranged from friends we knew who would be on their own and therefore possibly quite lonely, or international students that would not have the ability to get home to their family or anywhere else to go to spend Christmas Day. It was time to do the annual Christmas shop to make sure we would have a turkey and all the trimmings for Christmas.

I parked the car, found the nearest shopping trolley, and waltzed into the Sainsbury's store to do some festive food shopping. I wandered up and down the grocery aisles and dropped the essentials into the food trolley. The store was busy as was usual for this time of the year with everyone getting into the swing of their preparations and the aisles were crowded. Overhead, I admired the tinsel and decorations that sparkled as the bright lights caught the different angles. Then as I looked at the shelves in front of me, my eyes suddenly fell on the boxes of pink and white almonds.

The tsunami rushed in and then the floodgates opened as I choked and the warm tears flowed. Heart wrenching sobs broke out of my chest. I broke down and wept and wept. The painful feeling of losing my father enveloped me and I gave in to this huge emotional crash. Each year at Christmas I would always buy Dad his favourite sweat treat, pink and white sugar-coated almonds. I realised afterwards that grief trips us up and catches us when we are completely off guard. It is an excruciating emotion and not an emotion that you can speed up. What God showed me from this experience is that when we give ourselves permission to cry and shed those tears, we are processing our grief, allowing Him to start the healing process in us and there is nothing to be ashamed of or feel guilty about and that there is no wrong in doing that.

I found it ironic but was also filled with deep sadness now that I understood more of life, that as a growing child, I had never been allowed to cry if I was being punished by my father. If I did cry, he would hand out more punishment and that punishment was being beaten brutally with a belt. So very quickly, I had developed a learned behaviour that I was never to show my pain. Perhaps more about that at another time.

Over many years I have come to understand that broken relationships happen because we are all broken and we also live in a broken world. I challenge you to show me one person that has not experienced brokenness in their lifetime. Those disappointments keep coming and the events or relationships that cause us pain never go away. Sometimes we do not seem to be able to let go of them and they take up residence in our inner being. They change in the characters that are involved or the events that take place. But each time, they still sting with a tail that is long and with sharp barbs that inflict deep wounds and scars and sometimes even crush us if we let them.

Do you carry pain barbs and how do you manage them?

How do you react to these destructive scenarios when they happen? I know my instinctive way of always managing my own reaction is to either burrow deeper into myself into this bottomless pit or dark cave and bury the hurt, putting up walls or barriers to that person to make sure that they do not have the chance of hurting me again. To add fuel to this, I then grapple with how to forgive them. That was until God taught me another way, grace.

Each time I have experienced a traumatic event in my life, God has always been there and each time He has held me in His arms and gently shown me a new way forward. He has worked with me to strengthen my faith and to help me be strong and have courage to overcome my trials even when I have faced the darkest of days. God has shown me His abundant grace, always forgiving me, and loving me and He holds the same grace for you.

## THE HIDING PLACE

I do not know if you have ever read the work of Corrie ten Boom?

Corrie ten Boom was born on 15th April, 1892 in Haarlem in the Netherlands and she grew up in a devoutly religious family. Besides being a trained watchmaker, like her father, she enjoyed sewing and handcrafts of various kinds. These two facts helped me to feel a close affinity with Corrie as I have my birthday in April and because I love handcrafts of various types. But back to Corrie's story. During the second World War, her, and her family harboured hundreds of Jewish people to protect them from the Nazi authorities. Their family home had become a refuge for many Jewish refugees. Corrie and her entire family became active in the Dutch resistance and risked their lives. Then a Dutch informant told the Nazi's about the ten Boom's activities. When her family was betrayed, she ended up being arrested herself, along with her family. She ended up in the Ravensbrueck concentration camp, near Berlin.

She survived the war and set up a rehabilitation centre for survivors of the concentration camps. Based on her Christian values, her life of service launched her into ministry. Corrie travelled and ministered in more than 60 countries and in 1971 she wrote her best-selling book *The Hiding Place*, telling of her experiences during World War II. She was given recognition through many awards and accolades and this included being knighted by the Queen of the Netherlands. If you have not read this book and Corrie's story yet, I want to encourage you to put this on the top of your reading list. Her life of struggle and constant hope that led to victory during one of the darkest periods of our human history, is a demonstration of how her faith and courage and always holding onto hope, carried her all the way.

One of Corrie's best summary statements that resounds with such a strong message is that there is no hole so deep that our God's love is not deeper still. It says it all in a nutshell.

At times of my deepest need and darkest hours, I have reached out to God. It is at especially these times that I found myself reaching for my Bible and looking for those comforting and real promises. I know that I do this because He is faithful, His promises are true and He is always with me. Sometimes I get angry at myself that I only remember this when I am in desperate need or the deepest of traumas. But the one certainty I have is that He never judges me because He loves us and his love is unconditional. One of the promises of God is found in 1 Peter 5 and verse 10 [NLT]: *'In his kindness God called you to share in his eternal glory by means of Christ Jesus. So, after you have suffered a little while, he will restore, support, and strengthen you, and he will place you on a firm foundation.'*

Dear friend, I do not know what your pain or deepest trauma looks like right now, or the mountains that you have had to climb, but I want to let you know that we can have hope through the promise of His great love for you and for me. We have hope and that flame never goes out. This promise of God's is as real for us today as it was in the days of the people living in Rome that were experiencing persecution for their faith. That when the apostle Peter, who was one of Jesus's disciples wrote to them, he encouraged them and gave them this promise and assurance. This hope is as real as it was for the survivors of the concentration camps during the Second World War and as real as it is for the Ukrainian soldiers fighting against Putin's army in our modern-day war today.

I have climbed many mountains and found myself in the valleys more times than I care to remember. I also know that I am not alone in this and that many of you will have experienced a similar journey. You will discover more about these in the chapters that follow. No sooner do I reach the summit of one and I have stared another in the face. Through pushing on and pressing forward, persevering, I have developed a stronger faith and more resilience with each climb. None of these expeditions have ever been undertaken on my own. Even though I may have felt totally alone and even abandoned in some of these seasons, I have always held onto Hope.

No matter the decade and no matter the century, God's love for us never changes. Never let your hope go out, never let the enemy extinguish that flame of courage in you. It is all about hope, everyone is loved. Sometimes it may feel like it is a tiny ember and that there is no life left and all it takes is one light whisper from our heavenly Father and that ember can become a bright burning flame. In our darkest times there is always someone that is prepared to listen. I heard a saying once, *'Kiss the things that have wounded you because they take you closer to God.'* His banner over us is His unconditional love and grace. So, friend, be strong, in Jesus Name. You can do this with him by your side, even if you may feel that you are only clinging on by a thread. Selah.

# 6
# Colour amid Darkness

At that point in my life and as I sat in that Conference venue waiting for the keynote opening talk from Pastor Bobbie Houston, I felt that life was relentlessly beating me up. If I had been a boxer, it would have been like having gone 15 rounds at least 15 times over against one of the greatest boxers of all time, Mohammed Ali. This climb, step by heavy step up to this mountain ledge, had showered rocks on my head. My body was bruised, I was feeling pain and aching, and broken and I still had not reached the summit. *'How could God possibly expect or want me to sit up and listen?'*

Why had I not picked up the phone and called my father on that Father's Day Sunday? My father died at the age of 67. I felt robbed. It hurt so much. The ache in my upper abdomen was so deep and

I felt like someone was plucking my insides out. So much of this pain was my own sense of loss for his physical presence no longer being there anymore but also particularly because I had felt rejected. Every passing Father's Day after that fateful heart attack left me filled with guilt, pain and remorse and such deep and overwhelming sadness. I would feel like I was drowning all over again and could not come up for air. The deep blackness would engulf me. One key question I kept asking myself repeatedly, was whether I had allowed my pride to get in the way of reconciliation with my father?

Pride is a thief, a liar and destroyer. Had I been taught this lesson in a very ruthless way? I resolved to ask God to help me never to allow my pride to get in the way of any of my existing and future relationships again. I recognise changes I started making in my own behaviours and interactions. I know and could recognise that there were so many situations where I would expect things to turn out my way and then I would feel upset when they did not.

I felt dead inside, like I had no capacity to do anything. If I could not even help myself, how was I going to be able to help or support anyone else! But one thing I do know with certainty, is that God is a God of healing and restoration. Pastor Bobbie and her invited keynote speakers, modern day women of God, were bringing more bible truths and promises and I was hungry to hear and hungry to listen, really listen and be transformed. I knew even then in my broken state, that God has the power to heal even the broken and the crushed. You ask me how I know. This was not the first time I was walking this path of brokenness. It is written in His word. *'He heals the broken hearted and binds up their wounds.'* Psalm 147:3

(NIV). He renews our hope and heals our bodies and our minds. This was His promise that I had front and centre and was clinging to by a thread.

Have you attended any women's conferences or business conferences? What has your compelling reason been for attending? When did you attend your first conference and was it the experience that you had hoped it would be? Did you attend on your own or is there strength in numbers and did you decide to attend with a friend? Perhaps the location even had compelling appeal. Was it to grow your knowledge with the ability to learn from key note speakers or perhaps for the networking with like-minded women who were searching for the same solutions to problems? What lessons did you come away with in the end?

At this conference glancing at the speaker schedule, I knew that each one of these ladies have powerful ministries today and are authors, teachers, leaders in various fields, and are solid role models for our generation and those to come. On this occasion, they included Priscilla Shirer, Lisa Bevere, and Christine Caine. I sat attentive and alert for what was going to unfold. I knew how the Word of God when spoken out loud has the power to change us and I also knew then that I wanted to be found in His story.

I was thinking of the verses in Matthew 5:13 – 14, when we are told we are the salt of the earth and the light in the world. Pastor Bobbie spoke: '*I want you woven into a tapestry of love, in touch with everything there is to know about God. Then you will have minds that are confident and at rest.*' I knew I was lacking confidence and mental rest and I certainly had not understood the real meaning or significance of '*rest*' yet. I was about to learn. I was being challenged with how fruitful the Word was in my life.

How many times do you have to call your children when you want them to do something? I have found myself in this space when I called and called and got no response and until the frustration mounted and eventually, I got angry. That does not sound like anyone with any patience or grace, does it? I used to think that it also applied only to children. But have you ever been in a situation when you want your husband or your partner's attention? You call their name and get no response. Then you call their name again and still get no response and finally you go looking for them. I seem to find myself doing more and more of that these days and each time I feel the tensions bubble up inside of me and try not to get frustrated or angry. Occasionally when I am in a better mood, I will laugh about it. So, can you imagine how much our heavenly Father loves us to have so much patience with us? It is at times like these that I realise how much Grace He has and how little I have learnt and still need to learn and grow.

## ALL FROM A WHISPER

Have you ever heard a lover shout at the person that they are in love with, especially during all the tender moments of building their relationship when they fall in love? I do not think so. No. Tender moments of '*I love you*' are whispered, sometimes hardly audible as they gaze deeply into each other's eyes and with heads often bent close together. Like no-one else is around. They are caught in their own bubble and no-one in the world exists except the two of them.

They may whisper '*I love you*' repeatedly to make sure that their message was heard. Sometimes if they are separated in a crowd, their eyes may find each other across a room and they will quietly mouth the words '*I love you*' as they look intently and longingly at each other. Perhaps no words are even necessary. The look says it all. So why would we think that for God to gain our attention, that He would shout at us?

When I reflect on when God first nudged me and I heard that first God breathed whisper saying '*My child, I love you and I have plans for you, plans to prosper you and for you to be one of the workers in the field bringing in the harvest,*' I had no idea what it was going to entail. This was a loving father speaking tenderly to one of his children through a whisper, a God whisper. I felt excitement and nervous all at the same time. I realised this was something so much bigger than me or anything that I could ever imagine.

## INSEAD AND FONTAINEBLEAU, FRANCE

During my corporate business career, I was amongst a management group of directors in our company, to be sponsored by our Human Resources Division and Executive Management Team, to attend the very prestigious Insead Business School in Fontainebleau, France.

'*Insead is well known as one of the world's leading and largest graduate business schools which spans the globe. The diverse group of faculty members are from no less than 42 countries. It runs the broad portfolio of programmes for all nationalities, across boundaries, languages, and cultures with the purpose of creating new ways of doing business in the world today. Its main ethic is to be the driver of change through using knowledge, understanding, vision and tools to navigate the complexity of business environments. A key learning concept of the Business school is that we learn through the exchange of ideas and experiences.'*[6] https://www.insead.edu/

Attendance here was part of developing Directors from across the globe in preparation for taking up more senior roles and positions of leadership in the organisation. I had never imagined that I would find myself enrolled on this programme in 2016. It was recognition indeed, particularly because I am a woman and I was working in a Japanese owned Company. I had been told by one of my Japanese colleagues, that woman generally do not progress to higher positions in the corporate business roles as they are held primarily by men. Although we are living in a very politically correct society, there are still significant areas of discrimination that exist in other countries and cultures of the world and discrimination is still rife especially in the business world.

It is sad how cultures can place such limiting beliefs on us and the enemy is prowling and only too eager to use these as part of his lies to make us doubt our own capabilities. I am sure there are many of you who may have faced discrimination in one way or another, and it hurts. Not only does it hurt but it places limitations on who we may become and how we are treated in society. But I want you to know, our Heavenly Father does not discriminate. He loves us all equally and sees each one of us with the same love and grace in His eyes.

Have you been at the receiving end of prejudice or have you lived with prejudice in any areas of your life? How has it made you feel and what emotions and thoughts has it evoked in you? Has it resulted in you having to make some very hard choices and perhaps even meant that you have been excluded from something very significant? Perhaps like me, your battle has been one in a corporate business environment or career choice? The amazing truth is that God can turn even these situations around and defeat the enemy if we allow Him to.

Here I was, ordinary me and a woman in an executive role working in a Japanese company, being sponsored to attend one of the most prestigious executive business development programmes. When I arrived, it was to discover that I was one of only a handful of women on this residential programme of forty-eight members amongst all our work colleagues from multiple European countries.

During one of our courses, the course lecturer and tutor challenged us on limiting beliefs. As part of our group and individual assignments we were tasked with writing a personal letter to ourselves. This letter had to focus on what we believed our core belief system was challenging us with. We then had to note the top four items in this letter. The letters were then placed in self-addressed envelopes, which would be posted out to us a year post qualification and completion of the programme.

Imagine if you were asked to write a letter to yourself right now. Picture being given the topic as well and being told that the content had to focus on your limiting beliefs. If you are not sure what to include, think of any thought you have that you see as the truth and that then stops you from doing certain things. This belief that you have does not necessarily have to be about you. It could relate to how the world works, an idea or how you interact with others. Self-limiting beliefs prevent us from achieving success in our careers and lives. Examples include thoughts like '*I am not good enough*' or '*I do not have enough experience*' or '*this is not my time right now*' and the list goes on. The one thing they have in common is that they are toxic as they paralyze us into not taking those next steps forward or that one next step forward. So how are you doing? Have you identified a few of these in your own life?

I recall this same letter arriving at my address a year later and my surprise at reading the content when I opened it. At the time of writing, I had made a mental note of the four points and promised myself to monitor my own progress against these ambitions a year later. Yes, you guessed correctly, a year later I had already totally forgotten the letter. Here it was now staring at me. I took a deep breath.

And that is where my story started. I stumbled across this letter again when I came out of hospital. Coincidence you may say. This time when I took it out of the envelope and read it, there it was, in headlights and staring right back at me. '*How far have you got with your story? This is now a recurring theme and you must act on it!*' I really believe that God has an amazing sense of humour and incredible timing and no, this was not merely a coincidence. God is purposeful.

At that moment, I had to stop and ask myself the question: '*Why am I alive?*' I realised that God has me here for a reason and a purpose. I knew instinctively that I am here to make a difference. My life has meaning and I knew that my purpose is to help and encourage anyone who has struggled with various challenges in life or who is possibly still amid a struggle. He wants me to share the unconditional love that He has for us with you. Our lives are a gift. I had to go through all that I have experienced, to be able to share how it is possible to overcome our trials with the help of Jesus when we are prepared to rely on Him and let Him take the burden and carry us.

I remembered what Pastor Bobbie had written in her book *The Sisterhood*, (Pg249) '*Wear the mantle of your calling with ease – allow it to fall around you, and be comfortable in who you are.*'[7]. Without experiencing so many of the rockfalls or waterfalls in my life, *how would I be able to speak into the lives of others*, I kept wondering. Now, finally, years later I am learning that obedience to God is a non-negotiable. It has taken me time to grow spiritually and to recognise that it is about realising God pours out His Holy Spirit on us when we accept Him as our Father. He has focussed me now on what matters to others, so that I can rise and find my place in doing His work assignment.

## BE THE CHANGE AND THE DIFFERENCE

The theme of being the driver of change through knowledge and understanding equipped with tools – resonated with each of the Colour Conferences that I had attended for multiple years. One of the key themes and values of Pastor Bobbie's heart, has always been that we as everyday woman can '*Be the Change*' in our worlds, no matter who we are, no matter where we are. I made a God connection between this and a totally separate unconnected Stampin' Up! Conference in 2013, which had as its value statement for that particular year '*Be the Difference.*' The aim was to be making a difference in the lives of others.

God is the God of all creation and that also means of creativity. I came to discover how God was also going to use my creative gifts to be a part of His story. It started with the unfolding of a Stampin'Up! Conference in Frankfurt am Main with a conference theme of '*Be the Difference.*' My love of crafting had brought me into this world where I was introduced to Shelli Gardiner's story. Bound in the love of God, I found myself in two parallel worlds – of women gathering and meeting together. Lots of fun event activities, making new friends, meeting up with old friends and sharing creative makes with one another.

Meeting in Germany was such a treat. We had time to explore the Christmas windows with the advent of Christmas on the horizon, in a country where the Christmas theme included Jesus and His birth as front and centre, evident in the Nativity scene decorations in the shop windows. Whether the local people had a faith or not, Jesus was on display for everyone that walked down these streets and peered into these windows to see. A display which has God at the centre and centre stage. The other, an ordinary, secular space with a common thread and influence, cardmaking. The early cardmaking conferences had an event called '*CenterStage.*'

The ethics of the founder of this company, Shelli, were rooted in the love of God and Jesus. Who would have thought that paper could play such an important role? Then came Shelli's horseback riding accident – and faith, prayer, doctors' treatments, and surgery – but above all, the love and support of family around her and God's healing hand upon her life. It spoke volumes to the thousands of ladies meeting and coming together because of their common interest in card making. Shelli also said that she had named that conference '*Be the Difference*' because she had always held the belief that one person can make a difference. This belief is one that she seen reinforced over a twenty-five-year period as she had watched the crafting ladies making cards and making a difference in so many ways. She also shared how being the difference does not mean that we must always do big and elaborate things. She explained that even simple gestures matter too. A smile, a hug, a word of encouragement and a handmade card could have a huge impact in someone's life.

For many years since, I have used my card crafting to not only make cards but to bring a message of hope by sending them to people in my world. Sometimes it has been to celebrate happy occasions with them, sometimes to send a word of encouragement or to show gratitude, or other times to support them through loss and pain. I have discovered through God's teaching me to use my gifts that I have already been playing a part in His story, even before I was aware of it.

Each of these building blocks were additional steps in my development and growth as God was helping me navigate this path called '*life*' before me. More and more the understanding has become clear that my purpose is so tightly bound in how He wants us to serve others, being the difference maker and helping to bring about change in the lives of others. My focus has shifted like changing gears. Have you stopped for a moment to think about what the gear shifts are that have challenged you or changed your course in life?

We are living in a society that is so focussed on self and where most people are driven by the *'me, me, it's all about me'* culture. The price that is being paid is that people are inclined to not even see the person in need right next to them on the train or at the bus stop. Because so many people are living behind screens and/or hanging out on places like social media platforms, their lives are being caught up with posting only about the positives and hiding all the hurts and pains and struggles. They dare not be real. The social media platforms encourage a world where everything smells of roses. What is even more frightening, is how many people are starting to feel most comfortable now when they are living in virtual reality experience rooms and gaming rooms or games.

We are being robbed of human interactions and real-life friends and relationships because it seems much easier for many to be building these in the world of virtual reality and online gaming rooms. I know that God has used my creative gifts over years to also share my card making activities to bring light, friendship, community, and encouragement to ladies who also want to belong and build relationships and belong to a community. I have watched as their skills have developed and how friendships have formed in the group. It is so exciting that He is using my creativity applied to creating for Christ through my writing. It is so important to not lose sight of the human aspect and with God's guidance and direction, I am trying to use foundations from my past to help rebuild and restore where I can similarly make a difference in someone else's life. This does not happen in virtual reality.

Take a moment and consider this. Do you find yourself focussed on virtual reality characters, gaming rooms or virtual reality worlds or real human interactions and relationships?

Being the Difference rang in my ears and making a difference when the Russian war on Ukraine broke out and refugees starting arriving on English soil. As part of a Ukrainian outreach, I enlisted the help of a small group of my crafting friends. We designed and created handmade cards to provide a message of welcome when these people who had lost their homes, were separated as families, and separated from their support networks and friends arrived, could be welcomed with a message of hope.

When I started recognising all the parallels in these two seemingly different worlds, I was mesmerised afresh with how intricate God's plan is sometimes. If we take time to stop and observe what it going on around us, we can start to make connections and see the overlaps. It took me taking the time to be still and let God show me what He was wanting me to see. The threads of a tapestry all weaving together.

# 7

# Foundations to Rebuild and Restore

A valuable lesson I have learned is that every act of generosity that we share accumulates into something much bigger over time. Have you seen this happen before? We have responsibility in loving others, especially those impacted by wars, struggles and hardship. Today more than ever, we are caught up in the wars in our current day in countries like the Ukraine, Sudan, Niger, and Israel, to name a few. War ultimately affects everybody. Do you know any families directly that have been or are being impacted by the current day wars? I know that during the early 1960's my parents took in refugees fleeing from what was then known as the Belgian Congo. My late Dad and Mum shared their stories with my brother and I to help teach us that we should always recognise and see when there is need in others and to do whatever is in our power to help them and to do it with a compassionate heart.

Sometimes we discover or see that need in the most unexpected places and we have a responsibility to help. One such instance was when I was face to face with a severely disfigured, wheelchair bound, homeless person on the Champs-Elysees in Paris. I was in France again, to attend a training course and as our team wanted to explore a few of the landmarks of Paris one evening. We took a walk from our offices to the Arc de Triomphe, which stands at the centre of the Place Charles de Gaulle, also known as the Place de l'Étoile. (It is located at the western end of the Champs-Élysées). My work colleagues all passed him by as I stopped in my tracks. In that moment I felt my heart break and I also felt such disappointment in my colleagues. This broken and poor man was sitting begging and to them, he was a faceless person that they chose to ignore because he was a street beggar. I stopped, greeted him, and smiled. Then quietly I reached into my purse and placed in his stumps (of what remained of badly burnt, scarred hands) that he held out, the few notes I could find. Something in me changed that night. Internally I was weeping and bleeding.

How can we become so hardened, cold, distracted, and selfish when we are so privileged and are blessed with so much? Have you ever seen or found yourself confronted with this type of hard-heartedness during your life experiences? Today, it seems to be so much about 'me, me, me' with no or very little regard for the needs of those around us. I know that we cannot possibly do everything but I believe that we must do something. I think one of our biggest assignments is to follow the example set by Lydia in the New Testament. Her story is found in Acts 16:14-15 when she invited Paul and his companions to come and stay at her house, a selfless act of hospitality.

My work assignments throughout my business career saw me navigate multiple countries and cultures across the globe, as far reaching as Bermuda in the Caribbean, to San Francisco and New York in the USA, as far afield as Tokyo in Japan and Cape Town in Southern Africa. I recognise that they were all primarily about corporate work programmes and deliveries. There were so many opportunities to learn about different people and cultures and countries and each of them enriched my life in different ways. I can also see now with hindsight, that very little of my time was focused on what God may have wanted of me when it comes to building His kingdom. It fills me with heartache and regret. There are so many experiences and lessons learned during each of those visits, assignments and interactions with people and I know how I grew from many of those. There were many times when I saw God using me in small ways and working in some challenging circumstances and somehow it does not feel like it was nearly enough.

It highlighted to me that there are huge contrasts in life. I have witnessed and engaged with people with both immense wealth and extreme poverty. God has shown me that He can move in any of those places and in any of those situations. We are all His people and when we see such emptiness, depravity and hunger, the harvest field is huge. I knew then His whispering to me had purpose. His purpose was and remains to reach others and to share the story of His love for them with everyone that needs to hear it. In my small way I want to become His hands and feet in human form to help anyone around me that needs help.

## CALL TO ACTION

Over a period of at least a decade as I was called to sign up for and attend a women's humanitarian conference annually, I knew there was a God appointment waiting for me at each one. I could not afford to be absent. Each conference presented so many daughters of the King, each with such unique giftings and teachings. Each year I found myself hunger for more of what they were sharing and I knew this was God's time of really teaching me because I was making time to listen. Each of these amazing mentors have played a part in opening parts of God's word and teaching me valuable lessons in life that have helped also mould and shape me.

In some of their stories there were areas that proved to be relevant to my own life and to my journey to keep on the path that God has set before me. I have had to make choices along the way. I admit that not all the choices I made have had the desired outcomes I thought they would. Some have led me into dangerous places and some have cost me dearly. I still feel like there are days when I still pay the price for some of those wrong decisions and bad choices. It is only by His amazing grace and knowing that He loves me, that I can move forward with hope and joy in my heart.

I want to thank and acknowledge each one of these teachers that God has used to sow into my life. Some are pastors, some are preachers, some are teachers, some are missionaries and others are also famous celebrities. There is One who unites all of them, and He is our God. They include Bobbie Houston, Priscilla Shirer, Beth Moore, Joyce Meyer, Holly Wagner, Christine Caine, Marilyn Skinner, Lisa Bevere, Dawn Cherie-Wilkerson, Sheila Walsh, Dr Caroline Leaf. These are all daughters of the King on His appointed mission and our modern-day women of God. They have all had a role to play and an influence in my life by sharing His Word and His love and in helping me to take those next steps as I have continued to grow in my relationship with Jesus and my fellow human beings.

Are there any people that you see as spiritual mentors? What impact are they having on your life? There are so many new-age theorists and practitioners and I am always sad when I see people reaching for other solutions and answers, when God is right beside us.

One of the most impactful things I remember Pastor Bobbie saying was that *Colour* was a conference also referred to as '*Colour your World*' and that each of us had a God appointed responsibility to go home and to colour our world with God colours. How are you colouring your world today? Our world has become lack-lustre and grey and as women, we can make a very big difference. We have huge untapped potential inside us and all it takes, is for someone to believe in us and to draw us out of the safe spaces. All these speakers and teachers that I have listed here are godly women who have stepped out of their comfort zones to colour their world. If you are looking for inspiration, encouragement and finding new understanding and insights into how to navigate life with God on your side, I would highly recommend reading any of their books or finding their teachings online.

## SECOND GREEK TRIP TO RHODES - A NEW HOPE

A dear friend of mine was struggling and I mean really struggling. She had recently lost her beloved sister to breast cancer. With the pressures and stress of a corporate business role and the demands it placed on her and having to also navigate the latest trial in her life, things were starting to unravel and fall apart at the seams. I felt a nudge in my spirit and suggested to her that we take a short break together, somewhere where we could be away from the busyness, noise and stresses and find a change of environment and a place of peace. She agreed and we booked the short holiday to the island of Rhodes.

Have you ever found yourself in that place of desperately wanting to make it all better for a close friend and feeling a bit lost in how you can lessen their pain and anguish? How have you dealt with that situation? It is not as easy as getting a band-aid out of a box and placing it over their wound or a bandage and wrapping them in it. This time I was the person standing on the outside of all the family complexities that came with her sister's death and her family relationships and observing a deep rooted and complex pain.

The day of the flights and our departure arrived and our visit to the Greek island. We found ourselves surrounded by a group of summer holidaymakers all escaping to this part of paradise in the Aegean for the week. What I was not anticipating was the breathtaking beauty of the island revealing amidst its natural beauty, the simplicity of life. It was such a surprise to identify the contrasts of a materialistic, money driven society that we had arrived from, to a society that thrived on subsistence living. This was what we were to see and experience as we lived among the islanders for the following week that lay ahead of us. If you looked closely enough amongst the popular tourist towns and some of the resorts on the island, you would encounter that wealth in the popular playgrounds of the rich but fundamentally beneath the facade, the authentic islanders were full of the joy and laughter of life and life happened at a very different pace.

The experience of walking through winding, narrow cobbled alleyways, and the streets of Lindos, was unique in a wonderful way. Tiny shops with single entrances would open into a bigger shop inside and the multiple street cafés displayed blue painted tables against the backdrop of the white walls and blue fronted doorframes. Where there were windows, the wooden shutters were all painted in the same traditional Greek blue. One alleyway through the centre of the village had a strong and obviously very old grapevine. Its leaves formed a shaded canopy and the beautiful green vine leaves immediately made me hunger for a Greek dish of dolmades. Have you eaten dolmades or perhaps even tried making them?

Standing on the beach as you looked out across the bay, a few tiny fishing boats bobbed on the water like corks and across the vast, ink blue ocean I felt an incredible peace. A few unmanned fishing boats were turned upside down on the stretch of sand that I stood on. It was in that moment that I experienced an overwhelming sense of what the Apostle Paul may have felt and experienced when he met God in this sheltered bay in his quiet moments.

The total peace, tranquil setting, and beauty along with the stillness of that scene will always remain with me. This was the peace

I was wanting to share and wanted for my friend. I knew that it is only Jesus that can give us that peace if we are prepared to be still and wait to hear His voice and feel His touch. How was I going to share this message with her? I could not do this in my strength. I had invited her here; I believe prompted by the Holy Spirit. Now I needed to let God do His work in her. It was not for me to fix her. I had to relinquish control and know that God had it in hand

## THE VISIT TO THE MAIN CITY OF RHODES

Walking the paths of history and retracing the steps of the Crusaders was fascinating. Did you know that Rhodes is often referred to as the Land of the Knights? When you explore the history of Rhodes (as I loved doing because history is one of my interests), you will discover that it is also rich in understanding the Age of the Crusaders.

Between 1309 and 1522, more than two centuries, the island of Rhodes was under the rule of the Knights of the Order of St John and a sovereign state. It also formed a gateway between Europe and the Holy Land.

*The Museum of the Order of St. John shares the background and some of the history of this group of monks initially, who established a hospital in Jerusalem by 1080. They had as their primary focus that they wanted to care for pilgrims who had taken ill on their travels to the Holy Land. Then the men and women who worked there were members of a new religious order. It became officially recognised by the Church in 1113 and they were known* as the Hospitallers, caring for anyone and without excluding anyone irrespective of race or faith. After the Crusaders captured Jerusalem, the Hospitallers also took on a military role and they then became known as the Knights of the Order of St John of Jerusalem. The Order then moved to Cyprus for a short period following the recapture of Palestine by Muslim forces in 1291 and then in 1309, they moved to Rhodes. They remained on Rhodes until 1522 and then following conquests that besieged Rhodes, they moved to Malta.

Following the famous siege by Suleiman in 1565, which the Knights and the Maltese people survived, a new capital city, Valletta, was built. The Order's ships patrolled the Mediterranean and remained on Malta until 1798, until the island was surrendered to Napoleon. The original Roman Catholic Order still has headquarters in Rome; its full title is the Sovereign Military Hospitaller Order of St John of Jerusalem, of Rhodes and of Malta. Today it remains a sovereign entity in international law and it is still engaged in international charity work.[8] https://museumstjohn.org.uk/our-story/history-of-the-order/

To my surprise I discovered that it also minted its own currency and its main port rivalled that of Venice as a commercial port. The main and ancient medieval city of Rhodes is the largest active medieval town in Europe today, hence it is protected as a UNESCO World Heritage Site. The fortifications and gothic architecture built during the Crusaders' rule still encircles it today. The surviving walls run almost 4k around the Old Town. Each wall is about 12m thick and sometimes they are either doubled or tripled. All the walls are surrounded by a moat. (I remember seeing a real moat for the very first time when visiting Arundel Castle in England because there were not any castles in Africa.)

I loved walking across the stone cobbles of the Knight's Quarter and visiting the Palace of the Grand Master. *So, God, why was I here?* I found myself asking. It dawned on me that God had brought me back in history for a reason. But why this period specifically and why the history associated with the Knights and the Crusades? I knew there was a deeper significance and I chose to enjoy the atmosphere. God was teaching me stillness and in His time He would reveal more.

The key lesson for me, if I wanted to commune with God and hear His voice, was that I needed to be still. I was not going to achieve that easily in the busyness of corporate life, but I was going to find my Hope in Him in the quiet places and speaking with a small, still voice. It was my choice about making time for Him. Did I listen to that message and heed His voice? I thought I did but guess what, I am ashamed that even then, I still procrastinated.

It did not take me long before I was catapulted back into that corporate arena, driven my pressures to deliver, demands of managing teams of people, achieving results and being purely results and outcomes driven. Sadly, again God took a back seat and in the very back row. No amount of trying to convince myself that it was any different made a difference. I was only fooling myself. What was the result? It was inevitable that God would do what He always had to do to bring me to a point of listening.

# 8
# You are Unique

Have you ever stopped to consider how special you are? You are unique because there is only one of you. There will always ever only be one of you. When God created us, He did not use a cookie cutter and we were not manufactured on a conveyor belt in a factory being pressed out of a mould. He made each one of us different and whilst we may find that we have similar characteristics, looks or habits as someone else, we cannot be duplicated. Even twins or triplets each have their own specific traits or characteristics that make them unique.

There is another part to us that makes us unique and that is aside from our clinical makeup or DNA, we have a spiritual DNA. Your spiritual DNA is never really called that, or spoken of as broadly as people will talk about or refer to your clinical DNA. There has been a lot of press about clinical DNA, especially with all the genetic re-engineering that scientists are focussed on and evolving gene therapies. Very recently, the BBC broadcast a report that was also published in the newspapers, about the first baby born in the United Kingdom with DNA from three people after a new IVF procedure. The scientists and doctors proclaim that this procedure aims to prevent children from inheriting incurable diseases. I cannot believe that because of the progress with research on MDT, which is also known as mitochondrial replacement therapy (MRT), this led to the U.K. parliament changing the law in 2015, to permit this procedure. *If this is not humanity trying to play God, then I do not know what is!* But enough on that subject for now.

So, what makes up our spiritual DNA? These are the things that cannot be defined in a clinical laboratory or in a test tube. In 1 Corinthians 2:7-10 (NIV) we read: '*we declare God's wisdom, a mystery that has been hidden and that God destined for our glory before time began. …. it is written: what no eye has seen, what no ear has heard, and what no human mind has conceived, the things God has prepared for those who love Him - these are the things God has revealed to us by his Spirit.*' This passage in the New Testament tells us that there is a lot more going on in us and around us that we cannot see with our physical eyes. When we are ready, God reveals his wisdom to us through His Holy Spirit. I believe this happens when we reach out to Him and want to know more about our identity and have ears to hear Him when He speaks. We also must be willing to let Him speak. Our spirit is God given and God breathed and so your spiritual DNA includes your personality, your spiritual gifts, what your passion is and ultimately, your story.

Do you know the *Greatest Love Story* ever told? No, perhaps a good try? No, it is not a Hollywood great. I was challenged to be playing my part in the greatest love story, weaving my story into His story. Psalm 32:8 (NIV) *'I will instruct you and teach you in the way you should go; I will counsel you with my loving eye on you.'* Selah. These are the words God placed on my heart when I knew I was called to write my story by being me, warts, and all and to tell it like it is with all my imperfections.

Woven into the unique person God has made you and I to be, are the things he has designed specifically for both you and I. This is where our hope is found. Our life experiences make God's Kingdom real to others and knowing who we are in Him, allows us to understand God's call on our lives and be a part of that great story. Our stories, my story, your story, are all working together for good within His story. Our pain, suffering and scars point to a greater story. We must learn Who the story is about. Our aches become other people's healing. This is reflected in 2 Corinthians 1: 3 – 7. God wants you to participate in His Story wherever you are and with whatever you have. Every one of us is broken and every one of us needs God.

## A PLACE IN GOD'S STORY

A place in God's story is what came to matter more and more to me. I was hungering to know where and how I fitted into God's story. I knew that He has placed a call on my life. A pastor prophesied this over me and a spiritual mentor that was placed along my journey for several years before she passed away, spoke out the same prophesy over me. For years I grappled with what that really looked like and whether it even was a truth that had been spoken over my life. When I started hearing the small whispers all those years back, I knew it was not coincidental or my imagination. There was more to God's plan for me than the years spent in corporate businesses, doing the work that made companies rich. There were times when I know God was using me in the workplace but those times were far fewer than they could have been if I had been more alert to God's voice. I want to share one of these stories with you.

After experiencing my first cancer interlude, I found myself supporting a business colleague that had been diagnosed with very late-stage Leukaemia. We had been working as a small project team on a European assignment in Winterthur, Switzerland. The routine was that our small U.K. team would fly out from Heathrow in the U.K. to Zurich in Switzerland on the red eye flight every Monday morning. On arrival at Zurich airport, we would take a train through the lush green and picture postcard, mountainous Swiss countryside scattered with picturesque chalets, to the beautiful village of Winterthur. This would be our home for the week. We would undertake a return journey home on a Friday evening. This specific week, we realised that our one colleague was missing. Our thoughts were that perhaps he had missed his outgoing flight.

Later that evening as we all sat around the dinner table, our Program Head informed us that our colleague had been taken into hospital the past weekend after falling ill at home. The update at the end of that week was that our colleague was still in hospital and had subsequently been transferred to the St. George's University Hospital in London. At that point we knew it was more serious than everyone had initially assumed. Another of my work colleagues (and friend), and I, felt compelled to visit him and take something to help him pass the time in hospital.

With work demands we were challenged with a very tight timeline and families needed our time too, so it was only three weeks later that we managed to make the trip to London, armed with a DVD player and audio books. Alighting from the Tooting Broadway Tube station nearest the hospital, we made our way in the grey and the rain, the cold seeping through the warmth of our layers.

Once we established the ward, we could find our colleague on, we traversed the long, bleak hospital corridors until we finally reached the bright lights and the Nurse's station. To our absolute shock, we stood and listened as the Senior Nurse explained that our colleague was not doing well. Our visit would be very restricted to a few minutes only and only one of us would be permitted to go in and see him at a time. Stunned silence followed.

I knocked gently on the door and stepped inside. There in front of me he lay. His eyes were closed. He seemed to have shrunk and he looked fragile and almost lifeless, an ashen grey against the stark, white bedsheets. As I approached his bedside, he moaned slightly, his head turned towards me and his eyes flickered open as I spoke his name. I felt at such a loss. Gulping back a sob, my chest aching as though I had been stabbed. Words would not come out of my mouth at first and then instinctively, I laid my hand on his forehead and asked him if I could pray for him. He squeezed my hand and slowly nodded. I heard a whispered and hardly audible *'yes please.'* I prayed. As I prayed, I felt an intense heat flow from the palm of my hand warm against his forehead. I had never experienced that before but I knew that God had purpose in using me in that moment and in that prayer.

Three weeks later we had the news that our colleague had passed away. This is what his wife said to me at his funeral, and I quote: *'Dianne, I have never seen him look as peaceful as when you had been to visit him and prayed over him.'* I had not been aware that after my visit he had clearly had a conversation with his wife and shared with her that I had prayed for him.

I felt that for years my focus and time had been about deliverables in the business world and that I was being driven by a sense of having to achieve to be recognised and to be given a voice. Now I know that God chose to place me in this generation and that I was chosen for this generation. My one regret is that it took me so long to learn the lessons of where true value lies and how making a difference in the lives of others is far more important than any corporate deliverables or results. Sometimes I still struggle with why it took me so long to see that there was such an imbalance as I try to analyse why my priorities had wrong perspective. Then I realise that this has been part of my growth.

My assignment, to do what God has tasked me with, is in the here and now. God has taught me that once we understand our individual role in His story, life takes on a totally different perspective and the lens through which we view everything and everyone around us changes. The following scripture found in 1 Peter 4:10 (NIV) confirmed this for me: *'Each of you should use whatever gift you have received to serve others, as faithful stewards of God's grace in its various forms.'* I also learned that when God calls you it is the most significant assignment in life. It is far greater than any business work assignment could ever have been because it is about the life of someone else.

I recall a teaching from a Sunday service where the pastor said: *'Even if your story reaches one other person, that is person that God wanted to hear the message you have to share and that needed to hear it.'* It is not up to us to decide what God does with it. This is His work. It is our responsibility to be obedient to His calling. I have discovered that you cannot make a difference in the lives of others if you chose to do nothing at all. As you learn and grow and bring your personal and vulnerable self, the real and authentic you with your unique message into the world, you become a part of writing the story God has purposed and the world gets to see God's love being lived out in front of them. We become His human hands to lend that helping hand.

# 9

# You have Unique Purpose

Do you take time out to be still? What do you do and where do you go to escape the busyness of life that consumes us? There are so many times that God has nudged me into being still and they have not always been of my own choice. I find my life being interrupted and I must suddenly navigate where I have not been taken before. Come with me on another of these interruptions and see how I was brought to this place of rest and being still so that He could do his next bit of moulding.

Have you ever watched a potter and worked with clay in the field of ceramics or even been a potter yourself? I decided to learn about this craft many years ago. I was intrigued by a stunning ceramic urn that I had seen and was curious about the colour blends and textures in the surface of the urn – and impulsively, I decided that this was a craft I wanted to immerse myself in. If you have not been exposed to it before allow me to explain what it is. Pottery is a term used to refer to objects made by forming lumps of clay into structures of any shape that you may want to create. The clay is then heated to high temperatures (600–1600 °C) in either fire pits or brick-built kilns. This heating generates reactions that lead to permanent changes in the clay including increasing the strength and rigidity of the objects. You then have a choice to decorate these objects using various techniques.

By the next week I found a local ceramics course and enrolled to attend classes every Tuesday evening for a year. It was like going back to school. I was fascinated by it all, especially given my love of history and knowing that some pottery referred to and on display in museums today, date back to periods like (3100-2900) B.C or that earthenware jars were found from the Neolithis Majiayao culture in China, 3300 to 2000 BC. The lists go on when studying archaeological records. But enough history as I could write another book about processes and stages of pottery and all the archaeological connections across the globe.

The course was held at our local technical college. Our entry level work was hand moulding and building of jugs, mugs and pots using coils of rolled clay and a pinching process. As we gained more experience our tutoring evolved to working on a potter's wheel. We were taught about various types of glazes and paints and about different methods of firing our 'thrown' objects and one type of firing where the objects were placed directly in a fire. You would see these rough looking, dull, white coated objects being placed in the flames and covered over. Then they would be taken out after a period. Each one emerged with beautiful designs and each one totally unique. Its shape, form, and characteristics never to be reproduced again and each one a one-off, single production.

I believe it was no accident that I was led to enrol in this course and that God directed me into this area of study, as He directs our path in life. The broken shards of clay that are still being unearthed today each have their place in history and a story associated with them. I find it fascinating that many of the Dead Sea scrolls were unearthed and found in jars of clay. This ageless creative process, learning over time and experience has taught me two very significant life lessons.

God is The Potter. He moulds each one of us in His hands with love and extreme care. He pays attention to every small and intricate detail of who we are. He knows every encounter, action, choice, and decision that impacts our lives. We read in Isaiah 64:8: (NIV) *'Yet you, Lord, are our Father. We are the clay; you are the potter; we are all the work of your hand.'*

My first pottery lesson developed when I heard a message preached at a Church Conference by Bishop T.D. Jakes of the Potter's House Church in Dallas, Texas. I knew there was significance in his teaching and in this connection that God brought into my life. It was one of the dots in a collection of dots that was unfolding new teaching of the Bible for me. Following the message, I followed up by reading my first book written by Bishop Jakes titled *Woman, thou art loosed! healing the wounds of the past.*

God had not accidentally placed me in that teaching session because He never does anything by chance. Everything has purpose. It was then that I realised I was a broken piece of clay and that God was starting to put me together piece by piece. This primary message of this book was healing from the wounds of the past. If you have not read it, I would encourage you to add it to your reading list.

The opening scripture from the Bible quoted in the first chapter of this book, is taken from Luke 13 verses 11 and 12 (NKJV) *'And behold, there was a woman who had a spirit of infirmity eighteen years, and was bent over and could in no way raise herself up. But when Jesus saw her, He called her to Him and said to her, Woman, you are loosed from your infirmity.'* [NKJV]. I love what Bishop Jakes says in his opening chapter, describing how he sees the answer to all our illness. He makes the point that all people have problems but that God knows this and that is why God has a solution for each individual problem. He goes on to say that even though our problems may have been caused by something in the past, the solution now is a current word from God. We are reminded that the Word we hear today can heal our wounds from the past. How many of us wrestle with our infirmities of past physical or emotional traumas, tragedies, and disappointments in our lives? I was learning that our heavenly Father is the God of restoration.

The second pottery lesson was embedded in realising that each of us can be viewed as one of those clay objects. After we have been handcrafted, the next step in the process is the firing stage. Often, after our first firing in the kiln, we develop cracks and still have lumps and bumps that need to be patched up, sealed, or sanded before we are painted, dipped in liquid clay again and put back in the kiln. Sometimes He puts us in the furnace but when we emerge, we are an item of beauty and all the rough edges have been burnished off. There is a critical element to this stage. It is of being fragile and brittle and I can give firsthand account of this. I know that the times that I have felt like I am in that furnace, I have been experiencing a very vulnerable stage in my life and felt like the next adversity would push me over the edge and beyond a point that I would be able to cope any more.

Through these experiences and struggles I can relate to you if you are struggling. When our lives sometimes lie in shattered fragments on the kiln floor, He picks us up carefully in His delicate and loving hands and puts us together again. healing pieces of us, one part at a time.

## A PIECE IN GOD'S PUZZLE

The day has dawned grey and cloudy. As I lay in bed, I could hear the rain whipping against the window. *Well, do I get up or do I pull the duvet over my head and pretend I have not heard the alarm go off.* How many wintry mornings in the U.K. have you woken up and felt like the bed was too warm and inviting to get up to brave the day? I knew on this occasion there was work waiting to be done and that I simply had no choice. Work was not going away and I needed to get up and get dressed for the day otherwise I would be late.

As I started the morning my mind was wandering. I found myself catapulted back to the Women's Conference during the Spring. I had this image branded in my mind and I could still hear those mighty wings and as the dove came ever closer, the sound grew louder and louder and louder still – and yet with the spread of those mighty wings, it was the power of the Holy Spirit that was calling.

Suddenly my mind did a gear change and I could see that colourful, huge world map on the screen again. I remember wondering what lay in store for us and how the next speaker's message was going to tie into this world map. I suspected it was going to relate to all of us in the audience and that we were visiting this conference from various countries on that map.

## YOU ARE ONE UNIQUE PIECE IN THE PUZZLE

*I am a piece in the puzzle and so are you – in God's Divine puzzle*

The scene was set. There had been a great opening event of the Women's Colour Conference in London, followed by the welcome and opening talk by Bobbie Houston, founder of the conference. After the first morning session, we were filing into the stalls and boxes in the balconies of the Royal Albert Hall for the next encounters. It seemed so appropriate that as we were coming to sing worship songs to our King Jesus, hear teachings from the Bible by various guest speakers and testimonies and share in the love of the Holy Spirit and each other, that we would be in a venue fit for a King.

As we entered, the ushers were handing out a small puzzle piece to each of us as. I looked up as I had taken my seat and saw a large screen and the image of a Map of the World on the centre stage. *'That's a great backdrop'* I thought. For me it was a great representation of the audience that morning. We had all travelled from all parts of not only the United Kingdom, but also different parts of the globe.

A hush fell on the audience as Bobbie returned to the stage accompanied by a beautiful blond and petite lady. A few minutes later we were being introduced to Holly Wagner, our next guest speaker. Holly Wagner walked onto the stage. She was so tiny against the backdrop behind her and it seemed like she could almost be standing in one of the countries. What followed was her story. She was once crowned Miss Texas and so she walked on stage carrying her dazzling crown and then she started unfolding and unpacking her message. Hers was another life touched by cancer, but victorious, as she was here with us sharing her victory story.

Holly Wagner grew up in 3 countries namely, Venezuela, Indonesia, and England before moving to Los Angeles. She lived in Texas in the USA and shared with us the experiences when she had been crowned Miss Texas. She is a lady with a great sense of humour and she has a heart passionate for God and that is what I loved about her. She worked as an *actress* in films and television for over 10 years. She is also an author and a cancer survivor (and this is why I think I could identify with her instantly when she introduced herself on stage), international speaker, and the co-pastor of Oasis Church in Los Angeles.

She has lived and served in that part of the world with her husband Phillip Wagner, for more than 30 years. Holly is passionate about seeing women become who God has designed them to become. Through the women's ministry of Oasis Church, *God Chicks*, she has empowered thousands of women around the globe. One of my overarching thoughts captured from her talk were that: *'Small is mighty! The raw material of your life is a lump of clay and we are clay in the Potter's Hands.'*

There was a pregnant pause during her talk and she said: *'I'm sure you were all wondering why when you entered the arena, you were all given a puzzle piece.'* And yes, I knew this was going to be the 'AHA moment. *'Have a good look at the puzzle piece in your hand. Now that you have studied it, can you look at the map behind me and see where you think your piece fits in this puzzle.'* I studied the piece in my hand, then studied the world map, then studied the piece in my hand again. How amazing was that. I could distinctly identify the colour of my piece with the colour position on the large-scale map of the world. I could do even better than that. I could identify almost the exact location that I thought my piece fitted into. So, what was this little exercise all about, I wondered. After a few minutes, Holly then continued with her message and suddenly it all became clear and it all made so much sense.

I would not even attempt to give a full account of her message right now as I do not think I could do it justice. But here was my key take-away from it. Red, yellow, green, blue, pink, turquoise, grey and you can list every colour, I belonged in this puzzle. You are another part friend. My puzzle piece fitted and I know that if you were handed one, it does too. You may not know it yet and you may still have to discover this but I am confident that you will. The significance was that although I was only one piece in the puzzle, I was as essential as every other piece in that puzzle, to make it whole and complete. If any one of us did not place our piece onto that map, the map would be incomplete and it would not be able to function and serve its purpose.

Not only was I an essential part of this puzzle, but I was totally different to every other puzzle piece that each of us had been given. How amazing is that? God has made every single one of us unique. We all have a very specific place and each one of us serves a very specific role. As all the puzzle pieces are inter-locked and dependent on one another, so are we. Each one of us is inter-locked with the person next to us and for the whole body of believers to function. We are all needed. There is not one of us that is more important than the other. Neither are any one of our functions more important than the other.

I looked around the auditorium and as I recognised that we were from all different backgrounds, cultures, villages, towns and cities, sizes, shapes, and ages. I started to develop a greater understanding that we were all family. We are all part of God's family. What a privilege to know that He cares for each one of us and loves each one of us as His children. As Holly reached the end of her message, I knew that my life would never feel the same again. For the first time I felt connected to all my fellow puzzle pieces and I knew that wherever my journey was still going to take me, this message would remain with me always.

Sometimes God uses the smallest and simplest of images to teach us lessons and give us understanding. As a child I had grown up spending many hours building puzzles. It had been a real love of mine because I would often spend many solitary hours on my own. God had chosen a childhood love of mine to teach me one of the deepest lessons in life. I realised that whilst I had often felt guilty about not having read the Bible from cover to cover or read every book in the Bible, guilt had no place. God loves me all the same and He can teach me, as He can teach you, in the very ordinary things in life that surround us. Satan tries to guilt us sometimes into thinking that we are not good enough, as I had felt for many years that I was not good enough, but God had showed me I was. I was good enough, more than good enough. I belonged and He has given me a place where I can see that I belong and that has given me an eternal Hope.

We are all woven into a tapestry of Love and bound by a scarlet cord that runs through our fibre. Our greatest hope is that the scarlet cord is the blood of Jesus that was shed on the cross to give us eternal life if we accept Him as Lord of our life. I must share this message that Pastor Bobbie Houston shared in one of her books when she describes life as a tapestry with all of us the interwoven threads. She encourages us by sharing that we do not have to be scared. Instead, we must rise up and be who God has called us to be. We must be a part of God's tapestry of love.

## NEW BEGINNINGS AND A PROVERBS 31 WOMAN

Friend, if I have one request for you, it is to never despise new beginnings, no matter how small or seemingly insignificant they seem to you. Have you heard this statement before? *Where there is a small beginning, even the size of a mustard seed, there is hope.* I heard this message being taught once and it has become such an important theme for me to focus on. You do not know what God has planned and what God is doing next. Learn to walk this journey by trusting Him with each new day and each small step. This is a lesson I feel I have been learning my whole life. I was encouraged to become a Proverbs 31 woman. Proverbs 31:25: (NIV) describes this so beautifully *'She is clothed with strength and dignity; she can laugh at the days to come.'* Selah.

This is a promise I hold onto very tightly for my life as I know that the Holy Spirit will empower you and move you forward from wherever you are. If you feel stuck and cannot see a way forward through troubles, think of this promise and hold onto it.

Make a way and make time to have fun and to be able to laugh, by setting the days ahead apart. Commit each new day as you start each morning into God's very capable hands. It is a discipline and a conscious decision to make a choice and a decision to protect this time. A little bit like having your breakfast in the morning. It is time more precious that gold. Also be aware, as I have discovered on many occasions, that as you do this, the enemy will try and distract you and draw you away with various strategies.

There are days when I still struggle to keep up this exercise, but I keep trying each new day. I am committed and want this for you, to be committed to follow the best that God has planned for us. We can be encouraged by the message in James 1:4 (NIV): '*Let perseverance finish its work so that you may be mature and complete.*' Give heed to His voice and He will breathe new fire into your spirit. He will make your grain store full and you will feed His people. God has promised: '*so is my word that goes out from my mouth: it will not return to me empty, but will accomplish what I desire and achieve the purpose for which I sent it.* Isaiah 55:11 (NIV)

# THE STORMS OF LIFE - WEAPONS OF WAR

# 10
# Confronted by Cancer and Death

'*Ouch*' that really hurt. I was playing a ball game with my daughter and the ball hit me on the side of my right breast. I rather expected it to feel like I had been bumped. Instead, it was a deep, sharp pain that poked the side of my breast. A few days later, I was expecting the pain to disappear. It was not happening. I remembered being told by a doctor that it was always important to check our breasts regularly and to feel if there were any unusual lumps or bumps. It was not a practice I had got into really. Now, for the first time I found myself paying attention. I got into the shower and as I lathered soap all over myself, I decided to feel if I could detect anything unusual. '*Wowwww!*' I heard myself saying out loud as I felt this long, hard, cylindrical lump in my breast. '*Where on earth had that materialised from?*' Had I felt correctly? I ran my fingers along the side of my breast again. Sure enough, there it was. I could feel this hard, rod-like lump. At a guess it felt like it was about 3cm long and it was very painful as I pushed against it. *'Well alright then. Tomorrow I will have to ring the doctor and make an appointment to be seen.'* I said to my husband later that evening as I told him about the discovery.

*'I am going to send you for a mammogram Mrs Richardson. When we have the results, we can assess and then decide if we need to have a biopsy taken.'* A week later I had the mammogram at the Jarvis Clinic in Surrey. This was immediately followed by a core needle biopsy. Another week later I was booked in for surgery. *'Don't you love mammograms!'* They seem so brutal and yet play such a vital role.

Coming out of the anaesthetic, I remember feeling at my right breast. I could still feel what felt like my breast so I sighed with relief. The follow up appointment with the Doctor confirmed that I had a form of breast cancer known as *cystosarcoma phyllodes*. In my case the tumour had been classified as borderline. He explained that whilst the whole tumour had been removed it was not a certainty that it might not recur. I was 37 years old. How could this be happening to me? Suddenly I felt angry and scared all at the same time. Was this really happening? Did I hear the Doctor correctly? Now it became an imperative for me that I do my own research. I had heard of this happening to other people and even one of my friends, but this could not be happening to me. I wanted to know as much as it was possible to know and find out as much as it was possible to find out about this enemy, the *cystosarcoma phyllodes*.

*'Phyllodes tumours are a rare form of breast tumour; they can be benign (not cancerous), malignant (cancerous), or borderline (having characteristics of both). Phyllodes tumours account for fewer than 1% of all breast cancers. They typically need to be removed completely with surgery. They are less likely to respond to some of the treatments commonly used for breast cancer such as chemotherapy.'*[9] *https://my.clevelandclinic.org/health/diseases/24226-phyllodes-tumors Written by The American Cancer Society medical and editorial content team, last revised June 15, 2022].* This, in a nutshell provided the brief overview and outline of what I was up against.

Post surgery, I was called back to the hospital for regular ultrasound scans every 3 months for the first year after my first operation. Then it became once every 6 months for the following 2 years and I was told my next review would be another year after that.

We moved countries then.

It was bitter-sweet as we got on that flight that would carry us across the globe. We were leaving behind family and friends. A move across continents is no small feat. With the planning of this major life transition and with all the packing up and arrangements that needed taking care of and executing, there was very little time to consider health related issues. Our relocation date came and before I knew it, we had been living back in the U.K. for a full year. Time does not stand still and waits for no-one.

And then, history repeated itself. Memories came flooding back.

It was my mother that had tried to persuade my father to visit me in England when I was given my second cancer diagnoses.

Yes, unfortunately I had a second round of cancer and surgery as before. During and after my recovery, I knew I had expected and yearned for my father to visit me. However, I had not been willing to entertain a visit on his terms, which were to accept my Stepmother. I had still held the view that she was responsible for my parents' marriage breakdown and divorce. Even then my father was not prepared to get on a flight to visit us and to spend time with my family and I. It had left me feeling totally rejected. I kept questioning God as to what had I done to deserve this? I still felt as though I was being punished and that I must have done something wrong. I was totally closed to the idea and possibilities that there may have been another reason for my father not visiting.

I did not get it right then and sometimes I still trip up now, but I have learned and know that with God's help, I have come a long way in making the transition from always needing to feel justified in whatever my beliefs were. It has taken time to be willing to make the changes. I know I still make huge mistakes. I have learnt that having preconceived ideas can be very dangerous and in the same way, if we cannot have a humble heart, how can we expect to often hear what God is trying to show or tell us?

As my relationship with my father had been very strained, I had worked so hard on ensuring I had a better relationship with my mother. Many were the times she felt like my lifeline. She had stood in the gap between my father and I, oftentimes trying to bring reconciliation between us. There was so much she did not know and I would never have the courage to share with her either. Sometimes there are deep traumas that lurk in the past and they need to remain there. Buried and forgotten. Not all therapists or psychologists will agree with that statement.

# FAST FORWARD 10 YEARS

Fast forward ten years. As I sat in front of our family doctor, I heard myself telling him that Mum had been informed by the doctors in South Africa that she had Multiple Myeloma. I made an appointment to go and discuss it with him to understand more about this prognosis. He looked at me, stood up and came around to my side of his desk. '*I am so very, very sorry*' I heard him say. '*Multiple Myeloma is a form of blood cancer. It is probably the most aggressive form of blood cancer.*' I sat, lifeless. 'Doctor, what exactly does that mean? I do not understand.' Mum had not told me this and I had simply replied to her that I needed to talk to my own doctor to find out more about it. '*Well, there is very little known about treatments that have proven to be effective at curing it. The expected current lifespan of patients diagnosed with Multiple Myeloma is between 6 months and two years. There are multiple trials in progress and in one or two rare cases in the USA, patients have survived 5 years beyond diagnosis. Will she be starting her treatment in South Africa?*' he asked.

I walked out of his surgery in a daze, tears pouring down my cheeks. Through my blurred vision, I could see the surgery was full of patients waiting to be seen. It was Autumn and yet I felt like I was walking out into an ice cave. I shuddered and shivered with cold. Or was it shock?

Mum started her first round of chemotherapy in South Africa. My brother and I were having regular telephone calls, as I tried to understand more about the drugs the oncology team were administering. It sounded quite a cocktail. What really shocked me was the discovery that one of the drugs being used was Thalidomide. If you are of my generation, you may remember historically, that this was a drug given to many pregnant women during the fifties and sixties to treat nausea or morning sickness. It resulted in severe birth defects in thousands of newborn babies being born with limb deformities. Though the use of Thalidomide was banned in most countries at that time, it proved to be a useful treatment for leprosy and later, multiple myeloma.

A year later and after three extensive rounds of intense chemotherapy, Mum decided to move to England.

I was so relieved as I stood in the airport arrivals hall at Heathrow, and saw her walking through the exit doors after security clearance and baggage reclaim. Her frame looked frailer and her hair had gone almost white. How she had aged in the year since her last visit. As she cleared the barrier, I could not contain myself and I ran towards her, threw my arms around her, and held her tight. I could feel the warm tears rolling down my cheeks and my body rocked as I felt the silent sobs break lose in my chest. I was relieved but also so very scared. *'Where was my hope meant to be in all this God and where was my courage and faith?'*

The next five months were a cycle and a never-ending circle of hospital admissions and home visits. Mum would be admitted to hospital for about two weeks, then have a discharge which would see her home for about a day or two. Then she would be readmitted. She underwent a further two rounds of chemotherapy. Each of these were again different cocktails of cancer fighting drugs. The inevitable time came. The oncologists spoke to Mum and then to me. Mrs Richardson, your mother has decided that she does not want to have any more chemotherapy treatment. We must look at planning to have her moved to a hospice.

Two days later Mum was admitted to the Woking Hospice in Surrey. The oncology team explained that we would potentially see a remarkable recovery in Mum for the first few days. They cautioned us, as this period would then be followed by a very rapid deterioration and decline. I phoned my brother and explained all this to him. For the first two weeks I would spend the full days with Mum in the hospice and travel home in the early hours of the morning to get a few hours rest, returning to the hospice before the night staff would change shifts and hand over to the day team. My brother and I were talking daily. Then I moved in with Mum. I stayed at the hospice in her room with her. I would sleep sitting up in her chair alongside her bed (not that I slept). I would listen to her every breath and when she stirred, I would get up and make sure she was still alright and that she was still drawing breath.

Mum was sitting upright and I had helped rearrange her pillows so she could be as comfortable as possible under the circumstances. Her fragile frame was so small and she was the reflection of a skeleton covered in skin. It was hard to look at her and not feel shock and raw pain at seeing this suffering. She had withered away in front of me. Was it even possible that she could still be alive, I wondered as I looked at her. Still to this day, I feel remorse that when she had asked me to take her home, I had to explain to her that it was not possible. I had been extremely scared of not knowing how to manage her condition and frailty at home. The team at the hospice had advised against moving her.

She loved tennis and the Wimbledon match on centre court was Rafael Nadal playing Novac Djokovic. My spirit had lifted again and I was filled with hope. If she was able to watch the game and engage, really engage with it, then surely there was still a hope of her getting better and out of the hospice. I noticed she had slumped against the pillows and her eyes were closed again. Who was I fooling? She was so weak now that she was not able to support herself on her own. I pushed the television back into the corner of the room and made sure she was settled again.

As I stroked her hair, she opened her eyes and murmured to me. It had become increasingly more difficult to understand what she was muttering in the last day or two. *'Are you thirsty Mum? Would you like some more water?'* I asked. *'How can I help Mum, what would you like me to do for you? I want to be able to do something for you that you really need.'* Silence followed for a few minutes that seemed to last forever. Then her eyes flickered open and she quietly whispered to me in a voice barely audible. *'Please say Psalm 23 with me.'* There was a pause, then *'I want to say Psalm 23.'* Her request took me by surprise. I felt an element of fear grip my chest. Did Mum know that these were her last moments? Was she trying to tell me? I did not want to lose her, not now. I was not ready for this yet. I sat holding her hand clasped between both my hands.

Then, as she requested, I swallowed hard and slowly started with the words of Psalm 23: *'The Lord is my Shepherd, I shall not want, He maketh me to lie down in green pastures; He leadeth me beside the still waters, He restoreth my soul: He leadeth me in the paths of righteousness for his name's sake. Yea, though I walk through the valley of the shadow of death,'* I choked on the next words *'I will fear no evil: for thou art with me; thy rod and thy staff they comfort me. Thou preparest a table before me in the presence of mine enemies: thou anointest my head with oil; my cup runneth over. Surely goodness and mercy shall follow me all the days of my life: and I will dwell in the house of the* LORD *for ever.'* [NKJV].

The warmth of my tears spilling down my cheeks, I could taste their saltiness as we said the last few sentences together. Her eyes were closed and her breathing rhythm was slight.

I left the room for a short toilet break and when I returned, Mum had a minister at her bedside. He was reciting the last rites with her. Suddenly I was filled with anger. I demanded to know what he was doing. *'Your mother has asked me to come and pray with her'* he said. *'I will leave you with her now.'* When? How? Had she asked before and had he just arrived? All these questions flooded my mind. It all seemed so final. This was a very, very bad dream. It could not be real. It could not be happening. *'Medicine is not an exact science'* I kept telling myself and this minister certainly had no idea when Mum's time here on earth was coming to an end. I felt angry and resentful. *'Dianne, you need to hold on to Hope.*

*You need to hold onto your faith. God is a God of miracles and He knows the time and the place. Pray again, intercede for Mum.'* I was talking to myself and I fell on my knees again at her bedside and prayed. *'How can God be listening to me and answering my prayers when I feel so much anger right now?'* I chided myself.

The days and the nights blurred into one.

## DEATH ROUND II

*'Mrs Richardson, you really, really should think of going home. Even if it is for a half hour. Why don't you go home, have a shower or a short nap to catch up on some sleep. We will phone you if anything changes and you can come straight back again. You look exhausted and you need to take care of yourself too.'* The cancer nurse said. *'I think I may do that. I am shattered and I will be very quick'* I replied. I left the hospice car park in the morning rush hour traffic. It felt strange holding the steering wheel again. I was only on the road about fifteen minutes, when my mobile phone started ringing next to me. I pulled off onto the shoulder of the road.

*'Mrs Richardson?' 'Yes, it's me'* I replied. *'Mrs Richardson, I am so sorry.'* the calm voice at the other end of the phone said. *'It is your mother. She has slipped away, very peacefully.' 'No, this could not be happening. Not again. I was not there. How could she do this? How could God allow this now? I was meant to be there with her. Why had she decided to go now, when I had left her for only a few minutes. I was not going to be long. Oh why? Why had I*

*not stayed with her?'* I turned the car around and struggling to see clearly through my tears, I made my way back to the hospice as quickly as I could. My body was on autopilot as I drove the route and parked the car outside the hospice doors.

When I walked into her room, she was lying with her hands folded across her chest. The bedsheets were pulled up and tucked under her arms. She was so still and looked so peaceful. She was not breathing anymore and she was not moving. She almost did not look like my Mum anymore. Her face had changed. I kept staring at her through my tears for a few minutes, trying to recognise her familiar features. I reached out my hand tentatively and then I laid it on her forehead. She still felt warm. *'Oh Mum, Mum'* I leant over her, hugged her and the sobs broke free out of my chest. *'Why did you leave me Mum? What am I going to do without you Mum?'* I cried and cried until I felt I could cry no more. Then I sat and looked at her for a long while.

Eventually the nurse came in and gently took my arm and led me out of her room. I had felt the deepest waves of pain in the centre of my chest when I had lost like this before. Now this loss again. It wounded and it wounded deeper than ever before. I felt like I had a long deep knife being driven through me. Somewhere and from the silence, the following verse of scripture came into my mind from Proverbs 31:25 (NIV) *'She is clothed with strength and dignity. She can laugh at the days to come.'* I would hold onto this promise with all my might. I knew that I would not be alone. As I walked in the hospice garden, I noticed the beautiful pink rose bushes outside her room for the first time. Mum had loved roses. They were her favourite flower. I resolved in that moment to focus on the beauty of God's creation and felt a peace enfold me. I knew with certainty that Mum was suffering no more and that she was surrounded by beauty and peace.

In the months that followed I found myself questioning God about so many things. The second lesson in death I learnt was that when we are faced with death, we have a choice. As the person left behind, it is always the hardest. You can wonder around totally lost and you can drown in your grief. But there is another way too. You can choose to look at grief through a different lens. You can look at your grief through the eyes of the person you have loved and lost. How would they want you to be living each day forward? I had come to understand that in making the leap from living life before a death of a loved one, to life after a death of that same loved one, it would be a journey that no-one else could define or live on my behalf. I was the one that had to process all the emotions and find a path through it and beyond it. What brought perspective and made me be able to navigate the path before me, was turning to Jesus through it all.

I held onto Hope. I knew that with Him holding my hand daily, He was pouring His strength into me and giving me the ability to put that one foot in front of the other and to take those next steps. This was a journey of faith and having courage to make each new day exactly that. A new day and seeing it through a fresh pair of eyes. By starting a Bible reading plan, I was given fresh insight daily and my days were filled with promises of greater things to come. There was the reassurance that death is only a passing moment here on earth as we have an eternal life ahead of us.

I was being challenged by whether my fear was going to be stronger than my faith or whether my faith was going to be stronger than my fear. Let me share one of the promises I came across during that time of grieving, taken from Isaiah 41:13: (NIV) *'For I am the Lord your God who takes hold of your right hand and says to you, Do not fear; I will help you.*

## MOVIE SET AND NEXT ROUND

9/11, I was there! Do you recall where you were on that fateful day in history, September the eleventh? Well, we were not in New York but we were on American soil and in a part that was wrapped up in the events of September 11th. Unbeknown to us, my brother-in-law was in New York.

The excitement was mounting as more people filed in and filled the arena. Conversations were buzzing all around us. It was another early, American Autumnal day, with crisp air and beautiful blue skies and a sun filled morning. I could smell the waft of freshly brewed coffee from the lady's large coffee cup in her hand in front of me, as the streamlet of steam escaped. I do not know what I was expecting today at this MGM theatre, but it was certainly interesting and almost like a movie set. *That is quite natural really given that you are actually in the Disney theme park and that this is the MGM studio feature. Silly me.* Each scene we had passed as we walked around the MGM studios for the preceding half hour once we had alighted from our Disney Coach and before entering the auditorium, took you back to a movie set or a different movie scene. I felt like I had walked onto a film set.

The stage hands were pacing around on the Centre stage of the arena. Someone moved a few stage props and then disappeared. Still the anticipation was building. What was going to happen next? I checked my watch. *Not long to go now.* The music had started. It was quite dramatic. I recognised it as the theme from the Indiana Jones series. *Any moment now* I thought. Suddenly there was a shuffling, gasping and some exchanges happening behind us in the audience and then to the right of us and suddenly someone shouted '*The world is under attack. We are under attack.*' He was a tall chap and he was standing on his seat. He had a mobile phone in his hand. '*An aircraft has flown into one of the Twin Towers, and there's apparently another one that's flown into Washington.*' I looked at the stage where there was a small gathering now of 4 people all huddled in the centre.

What was going on? Was this the actual performance starting? It must be because we were sitting in the MGM theatre arena after all. Then the one person on stage started speaking into their microphone. '*Ladies and Gentlemen, guests, we have a very serious announcement to make. There are some world-threatening events happening right now. We are having to cancel our performance and clear the whole park. Please can we ask that you all remain seated and calm. We will be escorting each row from the arena and request that you follow your guides back to the coaches. Please do not panic and please help anyone around you that may need assistance. If we all do this in an orderly fashion, no-one will get injured. Your coaches will drive you back to your respective hotels. Once you arrive there you will be given further updates and instructions. Please be assured that we will also provide you all with complimentary guest passes as you leave the park, for a future return visit to MGM studios at Disneyworld. We wish you all safe travels.'*

Surprisingly, everyone was calm but the air was a buzz of multiple conversations going on all around us. Some people were crying. Some were on their mobile phones. We started filing out row by row. We approached the entrance to the MGM studios Theme Park and I could see our coach number amidst all the other coaches that were all lined up outside the entrance gates. Hastily, we made our way through the gates, were given our complimentary passes as we exited, and then we were boarding our coach. As we got on the coach there was a small television mounted in the corner next to the front window. I looked at it.

As I watched I could see this tall tower with smoke and bright flames billowing from what seemed to be the mid-section of the building. Then from the left corner another aircraft was approaching. Surely this was not normal? No large passenger aircraft would be flying this low and right amid New York City centre. I could hear all the gasps and even a scream or two as people around me saw what I saw. The aircraft flew directly towards the second of the Twin Towers and then it crashed right into it. A fireball of flames and light flashing before our very eyes and the clouds of white and black smoke emerging.

The television cameras zoomed in and to my horror, I saw people jumping off the top of the buildings. They were falling to the ground like sheets of paper that had been thrown out of a window. I stood frozen to the spot and felt sick to my stomach. I could not register mentally for a few minutes that these were real people plunging to their death. There were no parachutes or ropes. These people were throwing themselves from the top of the building and out of windows, to their death, to escape the horror of the inferno and being burned alive. This was no MGM studio staging a performance at the Disneyworld Theme Park. This was real life in full colour and horror.

The plane's undercarriage emerged and I could hear the wheels being lowered. Looking out of the window across the aircraft wings, the wing flaps were being extended. Then we were on the ground and taxying along the runway. We had all been briefed before the landing that we would be escorted off the aircraft, via a separate route into the Terminal building. Ours was the second flight out of the USA since air-space had re-opened. *'There will be a lot of reporters as you emerge and we will try and shield you from having to talk to any of them as much as we can. Please do not feel obliged or pressured to respond to any of them. We understand the traumatic experience this has been and is for everyone onboard. Once you have been cleared through customs, proceed to the baggage reclaim and then you will have an escort assist you through the exit.'*

I thought that was where the horror ended. A week later I was back at work. I could not concentrate. My mind kept switching back to those horrific scenes I had witnessed over and over and over again, as the various news channels kept rebroadcasting all the horrendous September 11th tragic and world changing events that unfolded on that fateful day in New York and Washington. Could anything ever be more devastating?

I sat in the doctor's surgery and waited for him to share the results of the breast biopsy I had undergone recently. '*Mrs Richardson, we have now had the results to your mammogram, ultrasound, and fine needle biopsy and unfortunately, it is not good news. There is a new tumour. It is in the right breast again. I have referred you to see Mr Kissin, the consultant at the Royal Surrey Hospital again. He performed your last surgery four years ago if I recall correctly?*'

Have you ever been on a merry-go-round? Deep in the corners of my mind that is where I suddenly felt I was. Back on that merry-go-round. This could not be happening all over again. How many more rounds before you feel like you are totally drunk? Is this a dream? Am I going to wake up and find that I am in that cosy and warm bed or is this happening for real? Coming out of 9/11 so recently when each day felt surreal and like a dream, was I back there again?

'*Mrs Richardson, are you alright?*' I heard the voice saying in the background. This was real. I had heard correctly. '*Er, yes, I am fine,*' I heard myself echo back as my mind was still numb with shock. '*When will I be seeing Mr Kissin?*' I asked our doctor. '*… and will it be at the Jarvis Clinic or will I have to go back to the Royal Surrey County Hospital?*' I asked.

Less than two weeks later I was sitting in front of Mr Kissin again. The next week I was walking through the hospital doors for my pre-operation medical check and my breast surgery was two days later. I regained consciousness when I heard someone calling my name. My eyelids were heavy and I replied without opening my eyes. *'She is coming around, her SATS are low and so we have kept her in recovery a while longer. She is ready to come back to the ward but will have to remain on oxygen.* I could hear the conversation going on around me but my eyes were too heavy to open them. I wanted to sleep.

Soon I was being wheeled through the draughty hospital corridors and into a lift. When the lift doors opened, I opened my eyes fully too. I noticed that my one arm was attached to a monitor that was on the bed alongside me. I still had an oxygen mask over my face. The nurses dressed in theatre gowns spoke to the ward nurse as they wheeled me back into the ward bay. The monitor was plugged into the wall socket behind me. *'Welcome back to the ward Mrs Richardson,'* the friendly nurse said. *'How are you feeling and would you like me to bring you a cup of tea?'* I put my hand to my face to remove the mask and within an instant she was beside me. *'No, do not take it off Mrs Richardson. We need you to keep it on another little while. You relax and I will bring you that cup of tea shortly.'* And with that she disappeared out of the room.

Instinctively, my left arm reached across my chest. I had to know. I was scared. I had to feel whether I could still feel a breast on my right side or whether they had performed a full mastectomy as Mr Kissin had indicated may be required. My chest felt flat, totally flat. *No, surely it could not be.*

When the nurse returned with a mug of tea in her hand, I could not contain my anxiety. '*Sister, can you please tell me what they did in the end?*' I asked. '*Mrs Richardson I am sure Mr Kissin will stop in at the end of his list today and discuss the full outcome with you. I do know that he did not perform a full mastectomy, only half of the breast was removed.*'

She was correct. Later that afternoon Mr Kissin stopped in my cubicle. '*The tumour was the same kind as before. It was a Phyllodes, but quite extensive fronds. I think I may have described to you before that it is a fern-like structure with tentacles. I had to remove half of the breast. There will be no requirement for reconstructive surgery as the body will naturally form scar tissue which will fill quite a bit of the space over time. The right breast will of course be smaller than the left breast. I was not able to clear a safe zone this time as the tumour fronds were right up against your ribcage. I have already spoken to your Oncologist. You will have an appointment with him next week and then he will discuss the next steps with you.*' Once he left, the nurse encouraged me to try and get some rest.

Multiple consultations with the Oncology team followed over the following years. When the choice options were put before me, I made the decision to not undergo further surgery or radiotherapy. As there is also no known drug to date that can treat this type of cancer, I chose to not have any needless and pointless medications or chemotherapy.

Instead, I asked my spiritual mentor at the time and a group of Christian friends from our church, to join my husband and to lay hands on me and pray for healing for me. That was in 2001. I still undergo regular mammograms and a year ago had another biopsy. Praise God, there has been no recurrence. I continue to stand in faith and hold onto Hope.

# 11
# Rhythms of Life

When you think your health is safe, another dragon and a mountain emerge.

Bleep, bleep, bleep, bleep. I lay and watched the rhythm as my heartbeat tracked on the heart monitor.

After admission to the cardiac unit earlier in the evening, it was as though I could feel every beat of my heart rhythm. It was now Day 3 following my arrival at the Accident & Emergency Unit again. Was it only a fortnight ago that I had found myself in the same place? Only this time it was a Sunday evening instead of a Friday evening a fortnight ago. Already I was feeling a too familiar sense of Groundhog Day. When our doctor had given the instruction that he wanted me to go directly to the A and E unit and that he was calling the medical team ahead of my arrival, I sensed with a sinking feeling and a huge knot in my stomach, that all was not well.

He had ordered a new set of bloods and specifically a D-Dimer blood test. I already knew what that meant with my previous medical history of blood clots. He suspected that I had a blood clot in my body. *Well, perhaps this will explain the shortness of breath I have been experiencing. Would it explain the unusual chest cramping pains that I have now been having on a fairly regular basis for the past couple of weeks. Or was it longer? Oh, it does not matter how long it has been there. I am relieved I told him about the chest pains as I am due to get on that flight on Sunday.*

The phone call ended. There was nothing else I could do now. I walked into the lounge and went straight to one of the bookshelves. If I was going to the Accident and Emergency at the hospital, I knew it would probably mean a lot of sitting and waiting around. Idle time. No, I was not going to be idle. This time I was going better prepared. I knew I had my Bible app on my mobile phone and so without hesitation, I reached for the book that caught my eye and beckoned to me, took it off the shelf. Minutes later, we were in the car and my husband was driving me to the Royal Hampshire Hospital. The book title read *The Sisterhood* by Bobbie Houston. What was the significance of this book in particular?

Here I was, in a hospital bed in the Cardiac Unit instead of 38000 miles up in the air and on the flight to Canada. I was being sustained by God. If this was a trip to enjoy a holiday the disappointment would be real, but this was a critical journey to be with our daughter who was due to undergo surgery. What was going to happen about that now? I felt a huge sense of panic. She has no-one to provide support for her and the family and to help her and be there with her for her recovery and recuperation. *Why was this happening to me and why now, at such a critical time?*

Here was another powerful moment unfolding in my life unfolding and over which I had no control. Right now, I needed to be well. I needed to be with our daughter above all else. I felt helpless and weepy. I reflected on the brave face my daughter put on when I had to break the news to her that I had been hospitalised and would not be able to make this important journey. It did not seem fair. *Why was this happening and why now? God, you must help me here. I am finding it hard to understand any of the good in this right now. Where are you God? I need you now, I really need you to come through for me in this.* I knew deep down that all I had was my hand reaching out to Him for strength and the ability to cope and deal with what lay before me.

The blood tests had been taken. Two hours later another set had been taken. Next, I was being wheeled down the breezy and cold corridors to the Radiology department. Following the chest x-rays and further ECG's, instead of returning to the Critical care ward I was brought to the Cardiac unit. *This is odd*, I thought. *They must really be struggling with all the bed juggling that has been going on.* I did not think any more of it.

All the same covid restrictions were still in effect so mask wearing, restricted ward entries and of course, no visitors allowed. My husband had dropped a bag at the main hospital reception with all my essentials and a very kind nurse had bounced through the door with the delivery. I longed to be able to see my husband and hear his reassuring voice telling me that everything was going to be alright. The day was long, incredibly long and the night was even longer.

The next morning the Cardiac consultant appeared at my bedside, with his Cardiologist in training. '*Good morning, Mrs Richardson*' he said, as he drew the blue curtains around my bed. The questions were almost familiar now as I had been asked the same things so many times over by so many different staff since my admission to hospital. This time though, there were a range of new questions too. At the end of all the listening, he pointed to my charts with the ECG tapes (there were at least six recent ones in my file now) and said to his assistant '*see this, this is what a myocardial infarction looks like. It also ties in with the raised heart enzymes in the bloods*' and then they dropped into a further exchange about the anomalies represented on my ECG readings and blood tests since my admission. *A heart attack? Surely not.*

'*Mrs Richardson, has anyone told you yet why you have been admitted to the Cardiac Unit?*' 'No, doctor,' I replied. '*I am assuming it is because they are struggling with beds now given the covid scenarios on the wards.*' He cast a glance towards his assistant and then said the words that sent a shockwave rippling through me. '*Mrs Richardson, I am sorry to have to inform you that you have had a mild heart attack. We will be sending you for a CT-pulmonary scan this morning and we will also get you scheduled for an angiogram. Given your family history of ischemic heart disease, we need to be certain that you do not have coronary artery heart disease. Because we do not perform the angiogram here at the Royal Hampshire hospital, you will be transferred by ambulance to Basingstoke hospital as soon as a bed becomes available. In the meanwhile, we will take good care of you here.'*

The porter and a nurse wheeled me down the lengthy, cold corridors once again. This time I had a blanket covering my legs so I did not feel quite so exposed or cold. As we entered the CT unit, all I saw was this huge circular structure of a machine. It had a much larger centre hole than I had previously remembered. After injecting something into my canula and giving me instructions, the radiologist left the room and the procedure started. Quite soon it was all over and I was wheeled back to my bed on the Cardiac Ward.

Heart attack and a pulmonary embolism (blood clot) in my main pulmonary artery. What a life defining moment to be given this dreadful and quite upsetting news. Now it was starting to make sense. All the unexplained breathlessness, the chest pain and chest cramping, the severe stabbing pain in the back between my shoulder blades. I had not been imagining something was amiss. *'Father God, thank you for stopping me from getting on that flight.'* Even when we do not understand when things like this happen, I knew in that moment that God held me in the palm of His hand and that there was still every hope of a full recovery and a long life. My hope being firmly planted in God's ability to heal me. *'Mrs Richardson that could have been a fatal flight. You are very, very fortunate.'* The words rang in my ears. Did I feel scared? Yes, of course I did. Wouldn't you? Even with the human reaction of being afraid, I knew that I was not in this on my own or having to struggle or do battle on my own because God was right beside me. I slept peacefully and restfully that night.

As the following days passed, I found myself being drawn to pick up *The Sisterhood* book that I had brought into hospital with me. I was starting to get into a routine. Part of this routine was to read and study a few chapters in the book at different points during the day. *Why on earth had I taken this specific book off the shelf from the myriad books that we owned? Besides, I had read this book before.* I knew that it was Pastor Bobbie Houston's account of how the whole Sisterhood journey had begun and how the roots of the Colour Conferences had come into existence.

I realised this hospital admission was not going to be a one day stay either. Three days in, there was a sudden bustle of energy on the ward. The healthcare assistants came in and we were all subjected to the dreaded covid swab testing. A few hours later the nurse came in and informed us that one of the ladies in our ward had tested positive for covid and if we tested negative for covid, we were being moved to a different ward. The sorry saga of the musical beds started. 'Gosh, what bad luck' one of the nurses said, as she took my blood pressure and stuck a thermometer under my tongue, at the point when I could not talk or answer back. '*Well, I pray a bed becomes available very soon so that I can have the angiogram and go home,*' I replied when I could talk freely again. The new ward I had been moved to had another five ladies. I struck up a conversation with Maggie in the bed next to mine.

Maggie was in with heart failure and another lady in the bed adjacent to mine, Janet, had been admitted with a severe stroke. We spent the next few days sharing some of our life experiences with each other and I quickly realised that I was able to bring encouragement to them both. It seemed so natural to be able to talk to them about my faith and faith journey and how through God's strength, we can overcome even the most difficult of trials.

Days later, the ward nurse walked in armed with a tray and the dreaded covid swab tests again. I stopped mid-sentence *'Let's hope this is a routine test again,'* I said to Maggie. *'I hope so too!'* she replied. *'I think they have to test us every second day because we have been direct contacts with a covid patient'* she said. Covid tests all done, Maggie and I resumed our conversation where we had left off. A couple of hours later two nurses in full PPE came through the doors. *'Ladies, we are going to have to close this ward down'* one of them said. *'There's another case of covid in this ward.'* My heart sank in utter despair. This surely could not be happening again. Not only was I waiting to hear who the covid positive person was, but I also realised that this was going to extend my stay in hospital even longer again. Besides, I could be the patient that had tested positive for covid! *Where is your faith, Dianne. You know you have prayed for protection against disease and pestilence and specifically covid. It will not come near you.*

The penny was finally starting to drop. How can I have taken so long to realise and accept, that God has purpose for my life. He is the reason I am still here. Time to sit up and smell the coffee. God has called me to be the next and hopefully, better version of me, this time with a higher sense of purpose for what He wants. It was time for me to be doing His work and not to be focussed on my wants. It was time to make that choice, that decision to change the way that I have always thought. It was time to focus on His calling and to write His story. *'Yes, you heard me correctly. This is ultimately not my story, but His.'*

It started to dawn on me that many years back I had read a book by a Christian lady, Maureen Onions, titled *God peels an Onion*. Maureen had written her account of how God had worked in her life, peeling back layer by layer of her innermost being to help her heal, to move forward with her life. Now I understood how reading her experience was a demonstration of how God has worked in my own life. I am always learning something new. Another piece was starting to fit in the puzzle. God has worked at peeling back layer upon layer of my inner self in order that I may be healed and to move me forward to share His goodness and His love with others.

Again, it was being reinforced for me, how we all continually have room to learn and grow. I have come to realise and see how life is made up of seasons and how for every season, there is a specific time. We are taught this too in the bible, *'For everything there is a season, a time for every activity under heaven. A time to be born and a time to die. A time to plant and a time to harvest...* Ecclesiastes 3:1,2 (NLT).

As I spent time in those hospital wards, I realised the urgency of bringing in the harvest. We are living in such challenging times. Not a day goes by that we hear further reports of wars, famine, floods, earthquakes, murder, riots, and our planet being destroyed. I believe that God wants every person to know that He exists, that He loves each one of them and He has the gift of eternal life for each one of us, if we will only open our hearts and minds and listen. And, time is running out and the clock is ticking.

# 12

# The Word Anchors

I love the oceans. Having grown up living at the coast for a very large part of my childhood and teenage years, I feel like the sea is a very real part of the fabric of who I am. My grandfather used to work on the docks as a crane driver for many years. Each Sunday, there was a family ritual. Mum would pack a picnic basket. In it would be freshly made sandwiches, seasonal fresh fruit and two flasks, a flask of tea and a flask of coffee. We would hop in the car around lunchtime and drive down to the harbour entrance. Dad would then ask the harbour guard on patrol which berth my grandfather was at for that day's shift. Depending on which quay it was, we would pass so many boats, yachts, and fishing trawlers. Scattered on the dockside would often be a huge array of anchors and fishing nets. I had a fascination with all things nautical but these old and aften very rusted anchors would always draw my attention.

We would find the berth and then the respective area where grandfather was working that day and park up on the dockside. After a short wait, we would see him descend the crane's iron stairwell and he would appear at the car window. Mum would hand over his sandwiches, fruit and either a flask of tea or coffee. As we drove back, again I remember seeing some of these anchors looking large. It never ceased to amaze me how a single anchor would provide the steadying that a huge ore tanker would rely on. In stormy seas it would act as the lifeline for the full crew on board those huge and heavy vessels that were being tossed about like sewing bobbins, as they rolled about in the waves being ridden by white horses. An anchor is always a symbol of hope.

Fast forward a few decades and let me share a little about how my constant hope and anchor in many storms has been the word of God, the sword of the Spirit. I have so many special friends that I have been blessed with.

Beautiful Zana, or '*Mamzana*' as many call her, came into my life about twelve years ago. We were introduced to each other by my daughter, at the church we were attending at the time. I felt an immediate spiritual connection with Zana at so many levels. She is my beautiful and loving sister in Christ and from my homeland on the beautiful Southern African continent. We met while Zana was working and living in the U.K. She has since returned to King Williams Town in South Africa. Zana is always sending me encouraging scriptures, praying with and for me and one of her gifts, is being an encourager and a faith builder for God's kingdom. How blessed I am to have such a beautiful sister. Why is this significant?

Have you ever found it hard to pick up a Bible and read it? For years I seemed to struggle to do exactly that. Then I would feel guilty about not reaching into God's Word every day and the more guilt I felt, the less inclined I would be to pick up my Bible. I knew that I would find hope and so many stories in the Bible. I also knew that if I made time for God, I would give Him the time and the space to talk to me. Yet, even this was not compelling enough. Does this shock you? How could I deny God time? I would then struggle with what felt like a quiet rebellion. As Christian friends around me would share some of their struggles and how they were finding strength by spending time with God, it would leave me feeling even more isolated. It was a vicious circle and one I struggled to snap out of. My dearest sister in Christ, Zana, has always been an amazing example to me of a gracious woman and lady, who never ceases to make time for God and from whom I have learned so many life lessons.

Then it happened. After attending one of the Colour Conferences in London, I had been deeply touched by a powerful message delivered by Priscilla Shirer. She is the daughter of Dr Tony Evans (renowned preacher and teacher based in Texas, USA) and she obtained her Master's degree in Biblical Studies from the Dallas Theological Seminary. Not only is she a minister, author and appeared in films, she has been ministering to women on a global platform. Her message was based on us wanting to hear, really hear, the voice of God. Following the conference, I read her book *He Speaks to Me*.

Its main theme is about preparing yourself to hear from God. In the opening chapter Priscilla shares how as a child she remembers her grandmother always sending her older sister a box of new clothes and shoes. The result was that Priscilla would always get the hand-me-downs. Then she reached an age where she longed, yearned, to have her own special gift. A gift that was selected specifically with her in mind. She relates this to how we sometimes get used to always being satisfied with hand-me-down revelations about God and waiting for other to spoon-feed us passages from the Bible. Her challenge to the reader was that as we grow and mature as Christians, did we not want God to give us our own special message, specifically with our name on it? This could only become a reality if we knew how to listen for His voice.

That was a defining moment in time when my life changed. That single message became a life defining moment for me. I could not put the book down. Finally, I recognised and understood the significance of being able to spend time in God's Word and to listen for His voice. I realised how for so many years and through so many struggles, I was still trying to be in control. I was the one trying to manage the outcomes and I had so often been striving to do it all in my own strength. Then why did it take me so long to listen?

As I was receiving both quotes and verses taken from different parts of the Bible from Zana, they were now having a deep impact in my day to day walk with God. They often had the effect of prompting me and being that nudge that I needed, that it was time to make space for God in my day. As the years have passed, I have become better and better at having my quiet times with my heavenly Father. I learnt that God also speaks to us in so many ways. There are so many verses in the scriptures that have taken on a living, breathing life of their own for me as they have cropped up at various times and through multiple trials, painful experiences, battles, and hardships. But I have also learnt that God has spoken to me in preparing the way too through His word, sometimes long in advance before an event has even occurred.

Before the outbreak of the Covid pandemic. God had given me this scripture taken from Isaiah 43:19. (ESV) *'Behold, I am doing a new thing ..... I will make a way in the wilderness and rivers in the desert.'* This verse popped up in multiple places and during different weeks. I thought at first it was a co-incidence. Then after it was not only in my daily reading, but also in a message from Zana, then preached about in a Sunday service. I had ordered a journal for myself from the Eden Christian bookshop. When the journal arrived, this was the verse on the front cover and every page in the journal quoted this same verse repeatedly. I guess I realised that God was trying to tell me something. He knew that to make me see it He would have to make it obvious, very obvious and so He did. I love how God has such a great sense of humour too.

As we moved deeper and deeper into the early covid months, I would walk around some days and recite this verse over and over in my head to remind myself that God was the one in control. His promises are faithful and I knew with a great sense of comfort, that although the whole world was going through such dramatic events, God would make a way through it for all His children. Yes, I did lose a good friend, Anita Spencer to covid. I give God praise knowing that she is at rest in His presence for all eternity now.

Did you lose anyone special to this vile pandemic too? If you have, I want you to know that God has seen your pain and collected all your tears. You can depend on his tender loving care. How do I know this you may ask. Because it is written in His word. 'You keep track of all my sorrows. You have collected all my tears in your bottle. You have recorded each one in your book. Psalm 45: 6:8 (NIV). You are precious to Him and He wants you to know that He loves you. He will never leave or forsake you.

I love the gentle way that God teaches us. My recent lesson from Him was via a lady that was selling wristbands in aid of a mental health charity. I was visiting Bakewell in the Peak District with my husband. This was our first visit to the area and as I stood on a small bridge admiring the scene of the clear water rushing under the bridge, I was mesmerised by the sound of the rushing water cascading down. Then I found my attention being drawn to all the locks fastened to the bridge railings. The last time I had experienced this phenomenon was when I visited Paris and stood on a bridge over the Seine. Each of the locks had inscriptions engraved on them. In some cases, they were initials of couples or sentiments of loved ones to each other.

I was feeling quite emotional and sentimental as I wandered off the bridge and found myself being approached by a lady wearing a T-shirt inscribed with a charity logo. I wanted to avoid her but realised there was no room to manoeuvre. *'Would you please consider buying a wristband to support our work with Mind*' she asked. The first time I had heard of Mind was when I saw an interview with Stephen Fry and he shared with the reporter the mental health challenges he has faced and why he supports Mind. They are a mental health charity in England and Wales offering information, help and advice to people with mental health problems. I instantly knew that I wanted to support their work and a make a difference and so proceeded to buy two of the wristbands. Feeling immediately compelled to wear one, I slipped it onto my wrist without another thought.

A few weeks later I was experiencing a dark and cloudy day, mentally. I found myself fiddling with the band on my wrist and as I looked down, I read the words inscribed on it. *'Be You; Be Happy; Be Positive.'* In that moment God showed me that I had a choice. I could let the enemy steal my joy or I could choose to lean on God. We have the beautiful promise that He is our strength if we choose to have His joy. Nehemiah 8:10 (NKJV) '...*for the joy of the Lord is your strength.*'

# 13

# Psalm 23

The large anchor and key Psalm over my life. I think of it as my life's Psalm. There are so many of the Psalms in the Bible that have such depth of meaning that have constantly been sources of encouragement and strength throughout my life. Psalm 91: a Psalm of protection, Psalm 35: another psalm of warfare and protection, Psalm 27, Psalm 46, and the list goes on. But if there has been one constant scripture that has run as a scarlet thread through the whole timeline of my life to date, it is Psalm 23. It has been and continues to be a recurring thread throughout some of my life's key events. The more I reflect on it, study it, hear it taught and the more I explore it and grow in understanding of Psalm 23, I recognise how incredibly beautiful and relevant it is and how it is a true anchor of God's grace and hope in my life.

I want to share a few of those key events:

- At my baptism: In the message from my Pastor at the time, a Rev. Martin Holdt, he wrote this Psalm as the primary message in the opening page of the book he gifted me with.
- This is the Psalm our Pastor read and taught from at our daughter's dedication service.
- Psalm 23 were the last words I shared with my late mother as I spoke these out with her at her request before she lapsed into a coma. She did not regain consciousness again and died two days later.
- The powerful and comforting words of Psalm 23 were spoken and prayed over me after my third cancer diagnosis
- Messages preached through various church services and events that have been significant in my life, have had Psalm 23 at their centre.
- My journey of healing and restoration – this is the Psalm that when preached and taught at key stages when I am struggling badly, has constantly brought me to a new beginning and outlook on life.

I do not believe that any of this has been coincidence. Instead, I know that this has been God's constant guidance and reassurance over my life. Do you have any verses of scripture or passages from the Bible that hold deep significance for you? Stop for a moment and reflect on what they are and how they influenced the way you feel or go about your daily life?

Our hope and strength lie in the one truth that Jesus is our Shepherd. If we look at David in the Bible, he was a man that knew God's heart. David was first a shepherd boy before He became King. We have a Shepherd taking care of us and watching over us. He wants us to be a part of His flock. (Remember the story of Shadow the Sheepdog that I shared with you earlier in this story?) God wants us to rest in Him by lying down and being at rest so He can restore us. We do not have to be anxious or stress when we are resting in His care. If we continually want to be in control and take things into our own control, we do not allow space for Him to heal us and fill us with new strength. The most encouraging thing for me in Psalm 23 is that I know that He has my back. He uses his rod to fight off the enemies in this world that come against and He uses His staff to hook me back so I do not go astray.

After my pulmonary embolism and heart attack, we were prompted to visit Christian friends living in Derbyshire. I had reconnected with Terry and Jill Eckersley whilst still in hospital. We had agreed in our Facebook messenger exchange to have a telephone call. I felt God opening a new door. We had the joy and privilege of spending a fun filled evening sharing with Terry and Jill a couple of weeks later. Terry invited us to their church on the Sunday morning and so we made the journey and joined them at the River Network Church in Matlock. I knew that this was no accident and that God's hand was moving.

At the start of the morning service, I had noticed the bible verse on the screen as we walked into the hall. *Ah, that must be what Terry is going to be teaching about today.* As the morning worship and singing made way for Word to be shared, I was expecting a message to be taught with Matthew at the heart of it. Instead, Terry started teaching and quoting the first verse of Psalm 23. I felt the butterflies tumbling in my stomach and a warmth flow through me. God's hand was on me and I could feel the Holy Spirit. The rest of the morning God opened every line and verse of Psalm 23. How awesome it feels when you know God is near and very present.

There is a renewed confidence in me that God's hand is on me and has been all these years, every step of my journey. I find it amazing how when we are inclined to forget God's goodness, He has a gentle way of reminding us how very present He is all the time. It is clearly far from over and I now try and walk with Him daily. Shortly after our visit to Matlock and Derbyshire, I was reading an email announcement that had been sent to the church members of the local church where we have been planted for the past five years. The Pastor's message was to inform us of the passing of a very well-known member of the church family. I never had the privilege of meeting this dear lady in this life but I am sure I will in my eternal life.

I know God uses many ways to communicate with us. This was one of those truly significant moments. The lady in question had been another fellow cancer fighter. When she finally lost her battle and closed her eyes on earth, she was in full knowledge that she will open them in the presence of Jesus. I identified with her battle but realised how blessed I was to still be thriving after my battles. It was not the cancer battle that caught my attention as much as what one of her closest friends wrote about her as a tribute in her memory.

These are the moving and profound words written: '*Your story is possibly the only Bible someone will ever hear.*' I instantly understood. Jesus love always wins and death is defeated. If we love Jesus as our Lord and Saviour, we have a responsibility to share that compassion and love with everyone who will hear. We are all God's children and He wants all of us to come to Him. Jesus is The Good Shepherd of our lives. He will come and find you. What a good Shepherd we have. In Christ Alone, my Hope is found.

# 14

# Prayer Interludes

How many times have you heard someone say '*Prayer changes everything*,' and how many times have you heard the saying '*Prayer is the greatest weapon we have?*' Have you ever been running on empty and not had any more gas left in the tank, in your emotional tank? For many years I would always think of prayer as my last resort when I needed help and did not know what else to do.

A friend suggested I read the book by Peter Gregg about prayer. As part of my growth, I have come to understand more and more that prayer is the most important way that I can communicate with God. I know that I can pray anywhere, anytime, and any place about anything at all. It has been such a revelation also revisiting The Lord's Prayer. It is no accident that Jesus taught us how to pray when He gave us the Lord's Prayer in Matthew 6:9-13. How often do you pray? How often do you pray the Lord's Prayer?

I remember how I used to feel guilty about not praying. I also remember when I used to attend many church gatherings and when we were in smaller groups and having a prayer time. I would feel embarrassed and my heart would beat in my mouth when I knew it was nearly my turn to pray. I would be panicking about what I would say to God and how I would sound to everyone else in the room, because they all seemed to pray so well, such long prayers and sometimes such complex prayers. There would also be a few people praying in tongues. That would leave me feeling even more guilt ridden and insecure. Why had I not been given the understanding of how to pray in tongues? Did I even understand what praying in tongues was? I believed I had the gift of the Holy Spirit living in me.

The more questions it raised, the less I had answers and it would raise even more questions. Until I realised that my praying and prayers were not about what anyone would think of me. It was my time with God and my ability to talk to Him. I would build my relationship and get into deeper communication with Him. God started teaching me after so many years that we keep learning. I recognised that as Solomon had asked for wisdom and understanding, that was what I was lacking. I wanted more understanding which would help me apply more wisdom.

Prayer can be a very complex subject and yet it is one that can also be simple. I am sure that if there are any biblical scholars out there reading my story, they may even be horrified at my description of prayer. To me, prayer is about very personal conversations with God. Do you use WhatsApp messaging? I do. It is my current social media tool for talking to all my friends and to my family that are abroad. I like to think of prayer as my direct WhatsApp link to God. I can message Him and talk to Him any time I like. I also know that as you see the two blue ticks next to a WhatsApp message and know that it has been both delivered and read, any and every message I send to God instantly has two blue ticks next to it.

When I was given my third cancer diagnosis, a very dear friend and in a sense, my spiritual mentor at that point in my life, asked me whether I would allow people to lay hands on me and pray for my healing. I knew that many friends and my family had been praying for me. This felt so different. *Why had I not thought of reaching out and asking this of my church pastor and church family before? Was it because deep down in my heart and mind I doubted God? Doubted in the faith of my husband or some of these friends? Where was all this stemming from? Was it my own self-doubt and my own lack of confidence of how deep my own faith was? Was my faith too superficial and would God really hear me?*

All these questions plagued my mind. I was reminded that I had seen a book written by Joyce Meyer called *Battlefield of the Mind*. '*Now was the time to go and find that book and read it*,' I thought. It was another step in my journey and God teaching me to overcome doubt and fear. Joyce addresses areas around doubt, worry, confusion and so many of the feelings I was experiencing. Anger and depression. Why was I angry and who was I angry at and why? As I read the book, I started understanding that all these negative emotions were attacks of the enemy on the fertile grounds in the mind, in my mind. He could only gain the upper hand if I let him. Where was my belief in God in all of this? Where was my faith that had stood the test of so many trials before? What was my hope based on? Now was the time to take ground and I was going to depend very heavily on the support of my friend Fenella and my husband John.

They gathered as a small group, including one of our church elders and his wife, my husband, and my spiritual mentor. We met at our friends house that Saturday afternoon and after sharing God's word, I sat down in their lounge as they all gathered around me. Each of them laid their hands on me and then they all started praying. I felt the tears well up inside. I tried to bite them back but they simply kept streaming down my cheeks. The warm teardrops ran freely that afternoon.

I was given the five years all clear and officially declared to be in remission by the Oncologist at the Royal Surrey Hospital St. Luke's Cancer Unit. Those prayers were twenty-two years ago. Praise be to God. As I reflect now, I realise that when there are points in our life that we do not have the capacity to pray for ourselves, there is always someone that God places alongside you that will be willing to pray for you. All you must do is ask. God does not judge us and He does not ignore us. He loves us, deeply loves us. He is a God of miracles and as Jesus performed all those miracles over 2000 years ago, God is still performing miracles today. Our task is to stand in faith, hold onto hope and believe and put our trust in Him.

*'Dianne, I have more in store for you, so much more. You must take that next step of faith and get out of the boat with Me. I will not let you sink'* the God breathed words were ringing in my ears.

Will you let me share some of the significant verses that have given me greater hope and a heart for wanting to serve Him and serve others? This list keeps growing.

- **Isaiah 61: 1 (ESV)** 'The Spirit of the Lord is upon me because the Lord has anointed me to bring good news to the poor, He has sent me to bind up the broken-hearted……'

- **Psalm 68:11 (ESV)** 'The Lord gives the word (of power); the women who announce the news (publish) are a great host.'

- **Isaiah 58: 6-14 (ESV)** – our commission. God gives us gifts to unleash for His glory. He uses us and our primary purpose is building up others.

- **Proverbs 16:3 (ESV)** 'Commit your work to the Lord, and your plans will be established.'

- **John 15:8 (ESV)** 'By this my Father is glorified, that you bear much fruit and so prove to be my disciples.'

- **John 15:13 – 15(ESV)** 'Greater love has no-one than this, that someone lay down his life for his friends. You are my friends if you do what I command you. No longer do I call you servants, for the servant does not know what his master is doing; but I have called you friends, for all that I have heard from my Father I have made known to you.'

**Personal verses as promises from God:**

- **1 Samuel 10:6,7 (ESV)** 'Then the Spirit of the Lord will rush upon you, and you will prophesy with them and be turned into another man. Now when these signs meet you, do what your hand finds to do, for God is with you.' (a scripture that came to me while on holiday at Sun City in South Africa, Jan 2015)

- **Joshua 1:9 (ESV)** 'Have I not commanded you? Be strong and courageous. Do not be frightened; and do not be dismayed, for the Lord your God is with you wherever you go.' (first given to me in 2016 and multiple times subsequently)

- **Isaiah 43:19 (ESV)** 'Behold, I am doing a new thing; now it springs forth, do you not perceive it? I will make a way in the wilderness and rivers in the desert.' (first placed on my heart in 2017 and again every year since when faced with significant changes such as being made redundant from corporate job, selling our house, and moving our family home and then again last year when I started writing this book.)

- **Psalm 139:14 (ESV)** 'I praise you, for I am fearfully and wonderfully made; Wonderful are your works; my soul knows it very well.'

- **Isaiah 40:31 (ESV)** 'but they who wait for the Lord shall renew their strength; they shall mount up with wings like eagles; they shall run and not be weary; they shall walk and not faint.'

- **\*\* Acts 20:24 (ESV)** 'But I do not account my life of any value nor as precious to myself, if only I may finish my course and the ministry that I received from the Lord Jesus, to testify to the gospel of the grace of God.'

- **1 John 5:14-15 (ESV)** 'And this is the confidence we have toward Him, that if we ask anything according to His will, he hears us. And if we know that He hears us in whatever we ask, we know that we have the requests that we have asked of Him.'

- **Zephaniah 3:17 (ESV)** 'The Lord your God is in your midst, a mighty One who will save; he will quiet you by His love; He will exult over you, with loud singing.'

## GOD MAKES THE CHOICE; GOD SETS THE SCHEDULE and GOD DESIGNS THE PLAN

Do you find that there are certain images or pictures that speak powerfully to you at certain times? I discovered over the years, that imagery is important as a part of my learning style. I want to share with you one such image that is branded in my mind's eye. Have you ever felt that images conjure up strong emotion in you? I recall the emotion as I watched the videoclip of Jesus on the cross, with a crown of thorns on His head and His body broken and bleeding. It also connected with another image, one of a scarlet thread wound around the cross of Jesus.

In researching this thread that connects us, I came across this verse in Leviticus 17:11 (ESV) *'For the life of the flesh is in the blood, and I have given it for you on the altar to make atonement for your souls, for it is the blood that makes atonement by the life.'*

When sitting in that hospital chair, I realised that this image of Jesus on the cross, with His blood flowing from His wounds, was a picture of Him being the living sacrifice on that cross, for me to be saved from my sins and to be cleansed. He is the atonement and sacrifice for me through the sacrificing of His blood. It was no co-incidence that the very thing that landed me in hospital again was the disruption of the blood flow coursing through my body.

I want you to think of a tapestry. Do you know how it is created and how it grows? How the various threads are interlocked and intertwined as the artisan creates it? The scarlet thread is the blood of Jesus flowing and coursing through our lives. God, the Master Artisan has designed each one of us and each of our lives to interlock with each other and ultimately form one big picture. He has created one giant, living, breathing tapestry woven out of individual people. If you are right in it and looking at it closely, you may not even be aware of it, or certainly not be able to see it. When you take a step back and look at it through a different lens, you may see it with very different eyes and look at it from His perspective. It is only then that every intricate detail will become noticeable and you will be able to appreciate His perfect work. Selah. Time to pause and reflect on God's Master plan.

We are God's creation, a masterpiece. We have been made new in Jesus so that we can carry out the good things that God has planned for us even before we were born. We are part of His masterplan and purpose. Ephesians 2:10 (ESV) *'For we are His workmanship, created in Christ Jesus for good works, which God prepared beforehand, that we should walk in them.'*

# NEW BEGINNINGS - GOD'S PROMISE

# 15
# Setting Sail with Wind in her Sails

There she loomed on the quayside. Each step I took drew me closer and closer. As I cast my eye along the length of the quayside, it displayed structures that resembled sails. What a unique design and so well suited to this berth at the Vancouver international terminal. It was incredible to think that tomorrow we would be embarking and that this Celebrity Infinity cruise liner would become our home for the next seven days when we set sail for Alaska. This was a lifelong holiday I had always dreamt of and I could not wait to experience it. I was in desperate need to rest, let time stand still, feel part of nature and to regroup and rebuild my inner me.

For now, my mind was still dwelling on the wind in my sails when I experienced an altogether different encounter. '*Where would you like to spend today?*' my husband asked as we sat with a few tourist brochures spread on the breakfast table of our hotel in Vancouver. We had done a fair amount of exploring the day before as we walked many of the streets in the central city of Vancouver. One of the restaurant staff had suggested a visit to Granville Island and market or a trip to Grouse Mountain. '*Why don't we do Granville Market in the morning and Grouse Mountain in the afternoon?*' I replied to my husband. '*We have time and I rather like the idea of doing both and given my love of both window shopping and mountains, I'd love to do both.*' He agreed that it was a good plan and so we set about planning our day and transport.

As we stood at the base camp of the cable car that would transport us up the mountain, I could feel the butterflies in my stomach. It never ceased to amaze me how grand the scale of some of these mountain ranges are. The last time I had stood at the base camp of a cable car was when visiting the Alps. The day was clear and the striking, blue skies appeared even more electric blue against the backdrop with the hundreds, no, thousands of lush green spruce trees. They looked like an army of soldiers, so neat and rows, upon rows, upon rows as far as the eye could see. And then it was our turn as we stepped onto the platform and the next thing we knew, found ourselves seated on the Peak Chair lift and swinging our way out of the cable station.

What an exhilarating experience as we started the ascent up Grouse Mountain. Sitting in the chair lift, my legs now dangling in the air, a slight breeze was playing with my hair and the stillness and quiet of the majestic mountain and forests all around as I drank in the splendour and the beauty of all I could see and as far as the eye could reach. The chairlift tracked higher and higher and higher still. The amazing quiet was so noticeable and it was as though the whole world had been shut out and it was only my husband and I on planet earth. As we soared higher the verse popped into my head, Isaiah 40:31 (ESV) 'but they who wait for the Lord shall renew their strength; they shall mount up with wings like eagles; they shall run and not be weary; they shall walk and not faint.' I felt an urgent compulsion to look the verse up on my mobile phone Bible app and this is what I read as I tried to look for it.

'Go on up to a high mountain, O Zion, herald of good news; lift up your voice with strength, O Jerusalem, herald of good news; lift it up, fear not; say to the cities of Judah, Behold your God!' Isaiah 40:9 (ESV). I gasped and held my breath. I knew in that moment that God had planned this trip. It was no coincidence and He meant business with me on this holiday. There was no escape and I would discover He has purpose in everything.

'*Look, look John*' I said excitedly as I pointed to our right. We were suddenly skirting very close to the treetops when they opened to expose a large enclosed area in what looked like electric fencing. You could see a few large rocks and as John turned to look, we saw them. Two large grizzly bears. They were majestic and stunning. Their dark coats glistened in the bright sunlight. I was amused when I saw their snouts as they were a camel colour against these dark chocolate brown hairy coats. Again, I babbled excitedly like a toddler. '*It is real; their snouts are shaped perfectly John. Like the Steiff teddy bears I have seen in toy shops.*' I was fascinated to discover later that this was a refuge for endangered wildlife that had been established for these two grizzly bears and they were called Grinder and Coola.

As we reached the summit, we alighted from the cable car. There was a chalky path ahead of us and we were surrounded by the most breath-taking panoramic views you could ever wish to see. I had seen many canvasses and paintings of mountain scenes and beautiful spruce trees against backdrops of still more rugged mountains. The incredibly bright blue sky above contrasting with these rows and rows of mountain peaks and the various shades of green of all the fir covered mountain slopes. The vegetation was so dense that I realised why it would be almost impossible to spot any bears amongst the undergrowth. There were splashes of pinks, purples and yellow – mountainside flora. Species that I had not come across before. We heard shouting and laughter ahead of us and as we came into the next clearing, we could see the zipline to our left and a teenage boy was shouting towards his Mum and trying to coax her to *'let go and take-off.'* Looking at the huge drop underneath her I was not surprised that she needed coaxing to make the descent.

Walking along the pathway to the restaurants and the rest areas that were signposted on our route, John and I started walking at different paces. Rather oddly, I found myself being held back as I slowed my pace. There was a sudden sound of rushing wind that came out of nowhere, right in front of me. A dust cloud and white mist swirled, twirled in circles like a mini tornado as it danced towards me. I stood frozen and rooted to the spot. Then the most incredible peace descended on me. I knew it was my encounter with the Holy Spirit. His presence is here, I can feel Him near. '*Praise You oh my Lord, praise you our heavenly Father, praise You, I give You all my praise. I worship and love You Lord. Oh Father, how great are the handiworks of Your creation, how beautiful are the mountains and the valleys and all of nature that surrounds me.*' I stood in awe, filled with a warmth that did not come from the sun but instead from the Son. In that moment I understood for the first time a little of the awe and wonder all the Bible characters that experienced the Holy Spirit must have felt.

After some quiet time on my own, I proceeded onwards to the main floor of the Peak Chalet, Lupins Café, where I joined John and found him already tucking into his alpine burger. Now, well fed and watered we took in the last activity on the mountain, the Lumberjack show. It was great fun and highly entertaining, featuring a crew of champion lumberjack performers showing off their skills on the top of Grouse Mountain. The large outdoor set featured two logging camps depicting the early 1900's. The act follows where Johnny Nelson from the Green River logging camp prepares to battle Willie McGee from Blue Mountain to decide who is the best lumberjack. The show was fast-paced and fantastic entertainment. They undertake log rolling, a 60-foot tree climb showing incredible agility and strength and certainly no fear of heights. There is also a two-man peg and raker saw exposition, competition of axe throwing, and an exciting springboard chop. It was fascinating listening to the historic narration and how the lumberjacks would spend their labouring hours followed by these antics.

The next day and early morning we left our hotel a little later than the day before. The sky was the most vivid blue and there was not one cloud in sight as we walked down Hornby Street to the waterfront. Drinking in the new sights and smells, the day smelt fresh. It was a real surprise to stumble across the seven-foot Salvador Dali work of art *Dance of Time*. It is a large bronze sculpture which is intriguing to say the least.

When I researched it later, I discovered that the image of the melted watch is the most well-known and beloved of Dali's iconoclastic images and that he chose to portray this image consistently throughout his lifetime, beginning in 1932. In this sculpture he presents the fluidity of time. It is described in the accompanying plaque as representing not only time moving, but 'dancing in rhythm to the beat of the universe and that universal time knows no limits, dancing on and stopping for no man, history or even the cosmos.' I was transported to reflect on Genesis and the time it took for God's creation and on the verses in 2 Peter 3: 8-9 in the New Testament in the Bible when we are told that to God each day is like a thousand years.

As I snapped out of my reflection, there was that wonderful surprise as we catch a glimpse of the Celebrity owned cruise liner, the Infinity, docked in port. This can be no co-incidence that I have been reminded about time and that the vessel we will board also has a time dimension, namely, Infinity. I have never felt as dwarfed before as she towered above us at the Canada Pier. So back to the Cold Harbour Café it was again for a hot drink and Wi-Fi access and messages home to our daughter.

The heat of the day was tiring. Soon we were on our way again aboard the No.50 bus and this time to visit the public markets at Granville Island. The twenty-five-minute journey took us from Downtown Vancouver across the bridge to the island and then a short walk lay ahead of us. How fascinating to explore all the sights, experiences and tastes of Vancouver and Canada. Such a mix of cultures and such diversity of influences in all the creations by various artists. Finally, we found ourselves sitting on a bench at the ferry entrance to the Granville harbour. Here we sat and munched our way through lunch, consisting of German Bratwurst, a firm favourite from our years of having lived in Munich in Germany. I fed a few starlings and only afterwards did I notice a sign that had written on it *'Don't feed the birds!'* Ooops! Hopefully no-one saw my error.

I realised I was setting sail now with the wind in my sails. That Holy Spirit encounter on Grouse Mountain the day before, was unlike any experience I had undergone before where I felt God physically stop me in my path and give me His reassurance that His spirit is right inside me.

Towards sunset, everyone was aboard and we were out on the main viewing deck to watch the first blinking lights of Vancouver start twinkling as the ship sounded her compulsory horn and we pulled away from our berth. My mind wandered to my beloved teddy bear.

That pink Millenium Steiff teddy was suddenly front and centre in my mind. She (*I am allowed to call her a 'she'*) was the first ever teddy bear that I owned. As a child as I was growing up, I recall how I had always longed to own a teddy bear of my very own. I never did. Each Christmas I would hope that when I got to the presents under the Christmas tree, that my teddy bear would be there waiting for me. Sadly, she never was. When I was given my first cancer diagnosis, I was desperate for comfort and the first thought that sprang to mind, was a teddy bear. I would be able to hold it close to my chest and feel the comfort that I think all teddies give to the little people that they are bestowed on. When we returned from our holiday and cruise to Alaska, I was going to find my Millenium teddy bear. For some unknown reason, I felt like I needed to feel her comfort again. There it is again, the theme of time.

A couple of years later after our last house move, I rediscovered my pale pink teddy and I wanted to cry. She had now been eaten and chewed and broken in a few places and was in desperate need of repair. I felt a bit like that. No, I felt quite a lot like that. I felt like I had been eaten, chewed, and broken in many ways and in many places – and I was in desperate need of repair. Who was going to be able to put me back together again?

# 16

# A new Day and a new Era - Forgiven

Each of these battles and storms that raged in my life felt as though they could get no worse. Yet through it all I knew deep down that I had hope to hold onto and that I was never alone in going through them. God was always front and centre and He always is, in every life scenario. Why is it then that so many times I would feel lonely, so isolated and as though I was paying a price for all the mistakes I have made during my life and the different seasons of my journey?

As time has passed and I have been studying more of the Bible, God's Word, I have been gaining more wisdom and more understanding. The enemy uses guilt to convince us that we are paying the price when that is a blatant lie. He binds us in chains, chains that leave us feeling helpless, condemned and captive to past wrongs, accusations, and failures. Jesus has already paid the price for all our sins. When the enemy cannot succeed in his ways, he tries to break us down by guilting us, making us fear, fuelling our anxieties, and making us feel like we are not enough for our family and our friends. He creates the lie in our minds that we are not good enough for our employers, not good enough to ever reach our goals, not good enough! Never going to be good enough in God's eyes.

I am reminded that when I drop into these depths of feeling despair and helplessness, Jesus has come to set me free, to set us free. Jesus came to break our chains of captivity. God's intention for us is not to leave us bound by our past mistakes and failings and weighed down in chains. God has sent Jesus, His Son, to be a living sacrifice for us and to set us free from captivity. Friend, I have fallen into this trap more times than I can remember. It has been taking me years and years to learn and accept that God's love for us is unconditional. He loves us with the most perfect and beautiful love that you or I could imagine. This is why we all need Jesus and our own personal encounter with God's Son. Ephesians 1:7 (ESV) teaches us *'In Him we have redemption through His blood, the forgiveness of our trespasses, according to the riches of His grace.'*

Have you faced physical battles and storms in your life? Are you possibly even in one right now and struggling to see how you can possibly come through it and reach the other side? Do you yearn for a light at the end of the tunnel that engulfs you? Are you struggling with accusations that run through your mind and keep you awake at night? Perhaps they are personal circumstances, or relationships troubles or financial struggles or a battle with an area of your health? Does the enemy plant anxiety and doubt, fear and lies in your mind?

There is a very good book I would recommend you try and read written by Joyce Meyer titled *Battlefield of the Mind: Winning the battle of your mind*. (I referred to it earlier in the story). In it Joyce expounds on the subject of how our actions are a direct result of our thoughts. She goes on to describe that if we have a negative mindset, we will have a negative life. The great news is that opposed to this theory, if we renew our mind according to God's Word, we will be able to live the good and acceptable and perfect will of God for our lives. She describes how all the harmful and negative aspects like worry, doubt, confusion, depression, anger, and feelings of condemnation are all attacks on the mind. In her book she shows us how to focus our minds to think the way Jesus thought. After reading her book I had great encouragement to persevere with courage in facing my daily struggles with some of the battles that rage in my mind.

Now I see each new day as the start of a new era. I have come to understand that our lives here on earth are temporal and that our eternal life that we are moving towards is with Him, our heavenly Father.

One of my biggest battles until recently, was striving for forgiveness from people I love. The painful journey that I have been on has taken me to the absolute abyss of the ocean and depths of despair. How was I going to surface and come up for air this time when I could not breathe anymore. I felt totally overwhelmed, lost, and felt myself drowning this time. There again was God. As I sat in that service, bleeding inside and not able to lift myself I poured out my heart to Him. In front of me I saw the words on the screen and mid-sentence, these words jumped out at me in large bold white letters, '*I have already forgiven you. You do not need anyone else's forgiveness.*' In that moment I felt this huge mountain lift and as I stared at those words, my eyes filled with tears and I felt them shamelessly cascade down my cheeks. My Father has forgiven me, I am loved and I do not have to continue my journeying days on earth still filled with continued and relentless guilt. How amazing is His great love for me, how amazing is His grace and great love for us!

What I did not expect was to experience His reassurance in whispering to me again the next day through the most humbling encounter, my introduction to Kal-El. I am drawn to a teaching in the Bible, when in James 4:6: (NLT) '*God opposes the proud but shows favour to the humble.*' And in verses 7,8 '*Submit yourselves, then, to God. Resist the devil, and he will flee from you. Come near to God and He will come near to you…*' I was to experience God in a new way, this day that I met Kal-El.

That day after I felt my chains of guilt had been broken through the message on the screen the previous day, the message that spelt it out, '*I have already forgiven you, you don't need anyone else's forgiveness,*' was when I heard God tell me that I am forgiven and felt my release from guilt. I realised that by serving even in the smallest of ways, God was whispering to me, giving me the reassurance that I needed. All I did was followed the prompting that

God had placed in my heart, to reach out to a very rough looking, hooded, homeless person that had been sitting on a sidewalk in a country where I was a stranger.

God encounters always fill me with fresh faith and hope that we are loved unconditionally and that there is no need to carry baggage that the enemy wants to burden us with. I also thought of that image of the *fridgeman* and his message of taking responsibility for our own mental health.

# 17

# Proverbs 31 Woman serves

*'Serving, you need to serve! You need to write your story'* I could hear God's voice clearly in my head.

I could not get those words out of my mind. I knew God had been showing me the way forward while I was in hospital and those words after our journey to Derbyshire were now well and truly cemented in my brain. I realised that even if my story reaches and touches only one person's life, it can mean the difference between life and death for that one person. God was reminding me that every single life is important and matters to Him and every life is worth saving. I have a role to play even if it is to reach the one person.

So much was finally starting to make more sense. Now I understood why God had taken me on the paths of becoming humble in spirit. To straddle the road where I had been given so much of my corporate identity in the European Directorship of a Global Pharmaceutical Company. This was followed by serving front of house in a coffee cafe of a Farm Shop. I recall the shock registered on one or two of my friends' faces when they had casually stopped into the farm shop café, only to find out it was me who was serving them their teas and coffees, clearing, and wiping down their tables. I could hear the hushed conversations as they stared at me in disbelief. There I was, working front of house and in what they viewed to be a very low role in society. I felt compassion for them.

It was leading up to Christmas and the Good Life Café was full and buzzing with conversations. A group booking arrived and it was me who had to show them to their table and provide their menus. Suddenly, I recognised a few of the ladies in the group. It was a lady's group from our church. A couple of Rotarian wives were also part of the group. As I showed them to their seats and after the polite greetings, I once again felt their eyes boring into my back and heard the whispered conversations stop instantly as I turned around and walked back to their table. Expressions of guilt registered on quite a few of their faces. It was then that I recognised how people often judge us by our work identity. I was starting to finally see where so many of the prejudices today find their roots. It was hurtful. Perhaps I was also being very sensitive to their facial expressions and reactions. I had to stop and ask myself the question why it mattered so much to me about what others thought?

That evening at the end of my shift, I went home drained, emotionally drained, and physically exhausted. As I relayed the story of the experience that afternoon to my husband, he challenged me with: *'Why does it matter to you what they think Dianne? You are not defined by your job. I know it still hurts you that you were made redundant but it does not mean that you were not very capable of performing the role that you did and having the executive position that you held. Besides, your identity has never been tied up in your job. You know you have your identity in Christ and that is what matters.'* A sobering challenge.

He was right. God had been teaching me all this while and I was only starting to recognise, understand and realise that now. For so many years, actually a few decades, my identity had been tied to my corporate business roles. The roles brought importance and a recognition, a recognition I had craved from my earthly father and rarely been given. They are what I had used to define myself as. They had made me feel important, needed, and recognised. *'Well, I wonder what they would have said if they knew that I had also been cleaning the toilets and washbasins a few hours ago,* I replied laughing. *'You really have to see the funny side in life too, don't you?'* It also taught me that God has a brilliant sense of humour.

No matter what the enemy throws in your direction, God has your back. He loves you and will get you through whatever mountains you may be facing. *The Lion of Judah has your back. Although we have an enemy, God's everlasting love will never separate us from His love. Not our worries or our fears can ever separate us from Him. It does not matter how much the enemy hates us so remember to let God's love consume you. Learn to focus on looking forward, not to the left or to the right. Learn to dwell in His presence. You will trample of the enemy because God is your shield.* I realised it was now the time to draw deeper with Him, learning to spend time in Hs presence. Feeling his garment around us and hearing His voice of reassurance. The enemy cannot stop Him. We are under the shadow of the Almighty and under His wings we are safe. No matter what the enemy tries to bring in our lives the victory is with God and He continues to fill our cup to full and overflowing. The overflow is so much more that what any corporate job, title or role is ever able to bring you.

## WOMEN, HAVE SERVANT HEARTS!

As I re-read Bobbie Houston's Sisterhood book, I was catapulted back to one of the first ever Colour Conferences that I attended. Pastor Bobbie had spoken of the Proverbs woman described in Proverbs 31 vs 10 – 31, a woman with a true servant heart and one that served her family, her female servants, the poor and the merchants of the day and above all, she honoured God. One of the verses I treasure from this passage is verse 25 (NLT) which says: *'She is clothed with strength and dignity, and she laughs without fear of the future.'* What a beautiful promise. This tells of a woman who knows her worth and who does not fear taking risks or working hard. She is a woman who leads with kindness, speaks words of wisdom, and displays unwavering faith in all that she does. What a role model for us for today.

Another woman with a noble and servant heart is Lydia. To me there is such significance in her story described and spoken of in the New Testament in the Bible with particular focus on her servant heart. Lydia was living in Philippi, possibly a wealthy and certainly an influential businesswoman, when she met the apostle Paul and his companions.

One sabbath day, Lydia went to the river's shore and it was here that she met them. In that time in history, the Roman authorities of Philippi had designated it as a place of prayer and worship for the Jews. While others along the river may have rejected what Paul was teaching about Jesus, Lydia accepted it and she accepted Jesus as her Saviour as recorded in the book of Acts in the Bible. (Acts 16:14). We are told that God opened her ears to hear the message and she was the first gentile to be baptised. Her next action was to assemble her entire household, telling them what had happened to her, and she encouraged and asked them to believe too. After her entire household accepted Jesus Christ as Saviour and were baptized, Lydia invited Paul and Silas to stay in her home (Acts 16:15). Later when Paul and Silas were thrown into a Philippian prison, Lydia visited them and attended to their needs. Her house became the first meeting place of the European church.

What an example of servanthood she represents for us even today. She recognised how everything she had, belonged to God and how she had a new purpose in life and that was to serve Him. Her career had not stopped her sharing the story of Jesus with her family and friends and she was also not too busy to make time for hospitality to others. It challenged me with how little I had really shared Jesus with business colleagues and that Lydia's was an example I should be following. I also realised that it is never too late. Are you or do you find yourself almost scared or embarrassed to speak about your faith? You are not alone as I have found myself there often but with God's help, I am becoming bolder and finding it easier to talk to anyone about my relationship with Jesus and with God.

Part of my discovery has also been about understanding how women in the Bible had played very significant roles. There is the story of Lydia who led by Jesus and her love for Him, really was instrumental in the first church being started. Another example is the found in the story of the Samaritan woman at the well who meets Jesus. By approaching her, Jesus demonstrates His care for everyone, regardless of their social standing. She was so excited that she ran back to share the good news about Jesus with the people in her village and they followed her back to learn more about Jesus. So really, she was the first women to start evangelising in her community in Samaria. Is that not amazing?

As I sat and reflected on these two experiences of Lydia and the Samaritan woman in biblical times, I was reminded of how many women evangelists there are today such as Joyce Meyer, Bobbie Houston, Priscilla Shirer, Christine Caine, Lisa Bevere, Beth Moore, Victoria Osteen, and the list goes on. I knew what God was teaching me. Each one of these women had or have a voice and they are not scared or intimidated or fear filled. Instead, they are excited about their relationship with Jesus and they are being bold and using their voices to tell their stories in the context of God's story.

## MEET KAL-EL

I had come out of a Tim Horton's having bought a hot coffee and a craveable. In case you were wondering, Tim Horton's is a renowned coffee chain in Canada and their craveable is a toasted ciabatta sandwich with a filling. I was hungry and I am sure the cold had a big role to play in that. As I walked precariously and slowly along the sidewalk packed with solid ice, with a thick level of snow covering everywhere, the vice of the freezing Albertan winter temperatures caught me in its grip. I wondered how people survive these extreme cold temperatures when they have no shelter or homes.

Lost in my own thoughts, I noticed and then saw him slowly approach from the other end of the sidewalk. I had found a spot in the sunshine and was standing in it trying to feel warm. He lumbered towards me. At first, I noticed the man's rough and unkempt appearance. He was wearing a pair of camouflage trousers and a black hoodie, with the hoodie pulled up and covering his head. There were black knee pads on each of his knees. In his hand was a white plastic carrier bag and he carried a small worn rucksack on his back. He sat down as he reached the end of the sidewalk and slowly proceeded to open his plastic bag, with his partially glove clad hands. He reached into it and pulled out a plastic water bottle and a loaf of bread and I realised this was going to be his meal. In that moment my heart bled and I was so grateful I had bought the coffee and craveable.

I walked over to him and greeted him and then passed him the food. His face had been partially obscured by the hoodie covering his head and as he looked up at me to take the food, I realised that he must be of First Nations origin. '*Thank you,*' he uttered. I lingered and felt I had to talk to him. '*Where are you from?*' I asked, saying the first thought that came into my head. I was imminently aware of how homeless people were so often rejected by society in general and how people never take the time to talk to them or even make them feel like they are human beings. '*I'm from British Columbia, south of here,*' he replied. I was expecting the conversation to end there, but it did not. '*I'm from a Red Indian reserve, south of here*' he said. '*I have got a son here. I came here but then Covid hit – and now I am trying to get back.*' I was not sure what to respond with and so I simply said what came to me next which was: '*What is your name?*' I asked. He looked at me this time, hesitated for a moment and then replied: '*It is Kal-El. My name is Kal-El. But it is hard to remember and so people call me Rudi....and then he smiled for the first time. You can call my Rudi if you like.*' I introduced myself to him and then deliberately called him by his name Kal-El. '*Where are you from?*' he asked and I told him. '*I guessed you were not from here. I could tell when you first spoke.*' He said and smiled again. '*Where does your name come from Kal-El?*' I asked. '*My father was an artist, a painter. He always painted Superman, for the movies – that was his work he did. When I was born, he decided to call me Kal-El.*' he explained. He continued with '*I broke my leg three years ago. That is why I have these knee pads. The doctors at the hospital have said that my leg has not healed properly so this is why they have given me these kneepads, to help me get up.*'

With that, my lift arrived and so I thanked him for sharing his story with me, as I touched his shoulder and said '*Good-bye Kal-El. I will pray that you get home soon. God bless you.*' He smiled at me in return and said with a tender softness that suddenly lit his face and reflected in his eyes: '*thank you for calling me by my proper name. It was as though I felt the hand of God on my shoulder.*' I gulped as I walked to the car, fighting back the tears welling up and swallowing hard to clear the lump in my throat. God was right amid us and I knew Kal-El was going to be fine.

As we left, I could not get Kal-El out of my mind. I knew I had to find out what this encounter with Kal-El meant or why I had even had this encounter with him. I knew it had not been an insignificant or chance meeting. We had been in Canada for almost eight weeks and why had this encounter had such an impact and sense of importance to me. I could feel in my spirit that God was reaching out and teaching me another life lesson.

Here was the humblest of men, broken in his appearance and with the challenge of surviving these extremely freezing temperatures of minus 27 degrees C amid a Canadian winter freeze. He was homeless and physically almost helpless, with an injury that was inhibiting normal movement, hindered by an unhealed leg.

In that moment I realised with a fresh pair of eyes, that God does not stop speaking to us. We get so caught up in the busyness of life and all the distractions sometimes that we do not hear or we fail to have ears to hear His whisper. Mark 4:9 (NIV) instructs us when Jesus said '*Whoever has ears to hear, let them hear.*' Do you know that this is repeated in the last book of the Bible, in Revelation, seven times. Not only are we told about hearing but we are also told about listening. In Jeremiah 7:13 we are reminded that God speaks and we do not listen. He is always speaking to us and how often do we make sure we are listening for His voice? He speaks to each of us individually into each of our own individual circumstances too. We need to be making the time to hear Him.

I know you may be asking now, how on earth can I do that because it is one of the questions, I asked a long time ago.

I want to share a few of the steps that I have followed at different times.

1. I have set aside a specific time in the day when I can focus and have time with God and then prepare, by praying and asking Him to draw near to me and to speak to me.

2. There are times when I have signed up for Bible reading plans and followed them.

3. Time set aside to write out gratitude cards have made me stop and reflect and be grateful and give thanks in prayer.

4. At different seasons I have journalled my daily bible readings and written notes on what I have heard God say during those times.

I took out my phone and did a search of the meaning of *Kal-El* and there it was staring back at me, the description taken from the Encyclopaedia Brittanica. *Why is Superman called Kal-El? Superman's real name is Kal-El, son of Jor-El. The suffix El, of course, means 'of God' in Hebrew, with Kal-El defined by some as 'Voice of God.' Before Krypton's doom,*

*Kal-El's parents put him in a Moses-like basket, sending him down the Nile of intergalactic space until he landed safely on Earth.* https://www.britannica.com/question/What-is-Supermans-real-name[10]

Here I was again, with God whispering to me in that soft gentle voice. Through this interlude with Kal-El, I felt completely humbled and my heart hurt with pain for Kal-El. He had seemed so forlorn and downcast when I first saw him and it had surprised me how his expression had changed during my conversation with him. He had become animated and eager to share with me a tiny glimpse of his own story, in how his father had bestowed on him the name that meant so much to him as it was the very name that gave life to his creativity. I knew there was a depth of meaning there for me to reflect on and discover. It filled my heart with warmth to know that in those few short minutes I had been able to place value on Kal-El by taking the time to talk to him and listening to him. What was even more encouraging, was feeling God's hand on both of us.

Our heavenly Father was confirming to me that I was given a voice and a voice for a purpose. I knew then with absolute clarity that God was using me in that moment but He was also teaching me at the same time. He revealed afresh that my voice was to be used for His purposes in reaching others and that I am here to serve. As I reflected on this encounter with Kal-El subsequently, I realised that my experiences during the previous year and a half of working in a servant role had taught me to be humble.

As I think of Jesus, he started His earthly ministry from a humble position. He came into this world as a baby and was laid in a manger in a stable, surrounded by cattle and sheep, the humblest of beginnings. He also teaches us one of life's most important lessons, that to be one of His followers, we need to serve with him. *'Anyone who wants to serve me must follow me, because my servants must be where I am. And the Father will honour anyone who serves me.* [John 12:26] NLT

So, friend, I challenge you. Where is your identity established? How do you define who you are or what your purpose in life is? God has used my change in job roles to open my eyes and teach me, but teach me with grace. He has brought me into a humble role, followed by another to show me that for so many years, my focus was more about me than it was about Him. I have come to recognise that so much of what had driven and motivated me for many years, was my lack of accepting that I was not in control. I constantly felt driven to achieve for various reasons. Perhaps some of it was because as a child, my father always pushed me to achieve academically and then I was pushed into my sporting career, where coming second was not good enough. I was always told I had to be first. I spent hours and hours training and putting in the hours to make sure that I would achieve that first place and that next award, always to satisfy my father and gain his approval.

What drives you and do you always want to be in control to the detriment of everything and anyone else? By God's grace I have been taught that not being in control is one of the best places I can be. It took me many years to learn this valuable lesson and to understand that none of anything that I have accomplished or achieved has been in my own strength. God has always had me in the palm of His hand and He has guided, led, shielded, and protected me every step of the way. None of what I may have accomplished was ever done in my own strength but with His love and help.

# 18
# Step out of the Boat

*'Come Holy Spirit and fill me afresh with your inspired words. Help me to tell my story of your great love for me and for all those miracles that you keep doing in my life.'* These are the words I uttered as I grappled with how God wanted to give me a voice with all He has planted in my heart. I know that I have a voice and that voice is to proclaim the greatest *Love Story* of all and to tell how my life has been transformed by this great love of His. I have been challenged to acknowledge that if we retreat and do nothing and withdraw into silence, we are failing in the cause of helping others that are in pain or struggling or fighting battles and with deep needs. It is not a time in this generation to simply ignore what is going on around us and to step away and turn blindly from all the other media, proposed spiritual and mindfulness remedies

and philosophies, many which are spreading false information and hope. I have come to understand how vital it is to be grounded in truth and to build our lives on the one true God. Now is the time to step out of the boat.

He is the God of love and love is the balm for every illness, every sorrow, every brokenness, and every ailment imagined. Have you ever been in such dark places, feeling crushed, lost, and total despair and longed to be lifted and to be able to smile and laugh again? To face life head on?

What are the hardest and most intense struggles you have faced in your life? What are the mountains that have stood before you? Have you ever despaired at how you would even begin to take the first steps to start climbing all that stood before you to be able to ever reach the top of that mountain? Have you looked down and felt like it has been the deepest of gorges in front of you and a cliff face that you were ready to tumble off, grasping for a branch that you could grab hold of?

There is no greater cliff edge to stand at, than facing your own mortality and staring death in the eyes. I cannot begin to imagine what it must be like to walk the paths I have trod without having hope. That hope has not been about brighter days ahead, but it has been a hope of having the living Jesus in my life and knowing that He is my anchor. I know that with each struggle I have felt Jesus holding my hand and God calling me to stand firm, to have faith and to be courageous.

# NEW BEGINNINGS - GOD'S PROMISE

The Apostle Paul encourages us in this in his letter to the Corinthian church when he says: *'Be on your guard; stand firm in the faith; be courageous; be strong.'* 1 Corinthians 16:13 (NIV). Very early on in my battle, I bought myself a pink and white candy-striped mug with these words *'Be strong and courageous'* scripted in ruby pink across the mug. I love drinking coffee and so this became my daily reminder of where my focus had to be. I deviate I know, but are you also a coffee lover like me and have you got a favourite mug? What do you have inscribed on it?

Have you longed to be able to fly free as a bird again, ever wondered what it must have felt like to be Jonathan Livingstone Seagull? Have you longed for constancy and certainty during the greatest uncertainty? When faced with anxieties and worries have overcome you in floods, have you longed to see the sun's rays shining bright over you and feel its warmth embrace you?

Where is the lighthouse in the darkness? Is this not what we search for when we are in the depths of the ocean or lost out at sea? Have you yearned for peace and quiet and have you longed for and searched for hope and for answers or solutions? Are there times in your life when you have been desperate to be filled with strength and life again? Do you find yourself in one of those dark valleys right now? When your body has felt tired, broken, and lifeless who have you reached out to looking to find a lifeline during the storm?

Perhaps you been thrown into confusion and darkness and uncertainty, and found your very thread of life is being shaken. All those well-made plans, dashed against the rocks as the storm rages all around and the skies are black and danger echoes in every wave crashing and cascading over those same rocks. The foam of the waves almost resembling the frothing at the edges of your mouth and when the mouth of the storm threatens to engulf you and swallow you up. Where is your anchor in this greatest hour of need and how will you ever come through and survive this storm?

Are there points of intense loneliness in your life? Have you felt totally isolated like a lone seal floating on an iceberg in the Arctic. Emptiness and vast open spaces, nothing in sight.

The intense vastness and enormity of God's creation was no more evident to me than when I saw it stretch before me along the coasts of Alaska. It was my first trip to this remote part of the world. I had always yearned to visit Alaska as it held a deep fascination for me. I felt an urge in my spirit to see the extreme cold of a part of the world that was accessible within reason and that also harboured indigenous populations and some of nature's most beautiful resources, like killer whales and glaciers.

We had booked an Alaskan cruise to celebrate my 60th birthday. Although I have cruised to a few countries in Europe before and along a few of the Greek Islands, I had never considered a journey as far as the Alaskan waters. I was filled with child-like excitement and was not quite sure what the experience would bring. Did it disappoint when it arrived? Absolutely not. It must be and remains the most beautiful and significant holiday and trip that I have undertaken.

After setting sail from Vancouver harbour in British Columbia aboard the Celebrity Infinity vessel, our first stop was at Icy

Straight Point. Icy Straight Point was originally built as a salmon cannery. It is a tiny port and located on Chichagof Island outside the small village of Hoonah, Alaska. It is occupied primarily by Alaskans who are mainly part of the Tlingit people. The Huna Tlingit are the original inhabitants of Glacier Bay. When fur traders arrived on Hoonah's shores in the 1880's it meant that some schools, churches, and stores soon followed.

This rare opportunity to visit such humble and very hospitable people, provided a look at the Huna Tlingit culture and at a people that survive primarily through subsistence living and discovering the importance of salmon and subsistence fishing in the Tlingit culture. But one key memory that I took away with me from this Alaskan port, was the number of small wooden church buildings that were dotted along the mile excursion that we were taken along before going on our excursion to see coastal brown bears on the nearby Spasski River.

We also saw several bald eagles, some in flight and some perched high in the fir trees. Verses in the Bible came alive for me as I thought of the verse that tells us we can soar on Eagles wings: Isaiah 40:31 (NIV) *'But those who hope in the Lord will renew their strength. They will soar on wings like eagles; they will run and not grow weary; they will walk and not be faint.'* What a beautiful image of encouragement and message of hope to know that we will have strength for that new day. I always thought that the indigenous people were steeped in their own beliefs and probably did not know anything about Christianity. How wrong I was and another lesson in being humble emerged. Why is it that we sometimes make such sweeping assumptions about other population groups when we have not even made time to study their history or done anything to get to know more about them, their culture, or beliefs before deciding for them whether they could possibly have a faith?

I subsequently discovered that Hoonah itself has eight churches, of various denominations. It is the principal village for the Huna Tlingit people who originally settled at Glacier Bay, Icy Strait, Cross Sound, and the Outer Coast. Today there are four original Tlingit clans. These are the Chookaneidi, T'aakdeintaan, Wooshkeetaan, and Kaagwaantaan clans. Interesting too, is that numerous other clans migrated too, as have non-native peoples, or married into the original Tlingit community. The gem discovery was that Hoonah city has a small boat harbour. How appropriate that God was showing me through the beauty of this Tlingit people and subsistence lifestyle, that small boats have a greater significance. There are so many stories in the Bible that feature a small boat. The most significant one I identified (and it may be different for everyone) and that I want to elaborate on, is the story of Peter getting out of the boat and being encouraged to walk to Jesus on the water. Matthew 14: 22 – 33. What strong imagery to share the message of courage and encouragement and faith in Jesus. If you have not read it yet, I encourage you to.

On the same cruise I met another wonderfully kind, joy-filled and larger than life itself, friend and daughter of the King, Anita. Her and her sisters accompanying her on the cruise, were all Bermudans. I instantly knew this was a God connection and friendship, filled with purpose. I had worked on the island of Bermuda many years previously and so I could identify with this family's home. These beautiful sisters were on the cruise to celebrate Anita and a very special birthday, as my husband and I were celebrating one of my significant birthdays. We spent many hours enjoying fun times, creating memories, lots of laughter and fun onboard and a land excursion in Ketchikan together.

Sadly, our friendship was only to be for two years before Covid struck. We were scheduled to meet up in the U.K. as Anita had recently relocated here. I received the very sad news that Anita died because of covid. It taught me another important life lesson which is not to cherish friends and not to procrastinate. Covid was so difficult with so many casualties and heartbreak for many. Everyone I know struggled to navigate this global pandemic. Once it was here, it was suddenly too late for many.

How did Covid impact you or people close to you? Did you find that life as we knew it before covid has not returned to being the same or familiar anymore? Has it left you feeling robbed or cheated in some way?

*The big lesson here for me was to learn to step out of the boat* and walk on water. God calms the storms around us or the storms we find ourselves in. Keep facing towards Jesus and keep your eyes fixed on Him and not the things or circumstances around you, no matter what may be raging in your world or what trials you may be facing. *'That may be easy for you to say'* you may gesture, *'you don't know how bad my circumstances are'* or *'you don't know or understand the struggles I am facing or the challenges I am facing'* or *'you will never know where I've been and how I can never be good enough for Him to love me that he would want to help me or bail me out.'* How do I know that, because I have trod those paths.

Back to the Alaskan trip, I found myself feeling as though I was looking at God's creation through a new lens and seeing it in a whole new way. The sheer scale and vastness of this open land, ocean, a humble people, the bald eagles, and fishing boats were a reminder of verses in the Bible that have so much significance and relevance in my life. I was experiencing a closeness to God and being filled with His Holy Spirit that I had not felt for a very long time. I kept feeling a sense of awe, that our heavenly Father loves us so much and has so much grace for us all.

## SEASON OF OBEDIENCE

The nudges to write over the years, have been like a tide that flows and ebbs. Similarly, my motivation has ebbed and flowed. Then God changed the momentum and turned it up. Not one notch but a series of whole notches thrown together and I have been catapulted to the front of the class. In starting my new journey and season of obedience to God's calling, I am beyond excited to see what God can do.

Have you heard the beautiful words to the song that go *'it is no secret what God can do. What He's done for others He can do for you?'* I am standing in faith and reaching out and claiming that promise today. That what God has done for others, He can do for me and I know He can do the same for you in any of your circumstances. If He has done all this for me, He absolutely can do this and so much more for you too.

It is a deep yearning of mine to serve God through creativity in a way that will reach and touch the lives of others. I want to make a difference by helping other women who have undergone or are in the middle of struggles, like me. He has taught me that can only happen when I am prepared to be vulnerable and to share my inner thoughts and feelings. Who would ever want to expose the rawness deep inside them? It is only with the confidence of knowing that God has me covered that I feel I am able to have that voice.

I have admired the writer Allen Arnold after being introduced to his work earlier this year. His focus for his regular writing is story, God, and creativity. In his writings I was reminded that we have an enemy who comes to steal, kill, and destroy. We are warned of this is John 10:10 (ESV) 'The thief comes only to steal and kill and destroy.' Allen highlights how 'The enemy hates that we experience intimacy with God as we co-create together.'[11] https://www.withallen.com/blog/the-enemy-of-our-creativity, so he encourages us never to lose heart or to grow fearful, but to lean into God. I am leaning into God.

If I ask you to think about serving, what enters your mind? Is it being seated in a posh restaurant and having an enjoyable culinary experience and feeling like a million dollars because you are being served the most delectable food that you have not had to cook yourself? And bonus, you will not have to do the washing up because there will be someone clearing your plates and doing it all behind the scenes. Or do you think of going into a shop and being served by a shop assistant?

If you are in a church environment, serving is often associated with being a member on a team. I served on a prayer and praise team and then a coffee team (and now an international café team.) It was a wonderful way to welcome people that walked through the doors to church and to get to chat to them, and soon there were many familiar faces. Over time as I built relationships with them, it was so rewarding and such an honour to be able to share in some of their life stories and challenges and celebrations too. Sometimes it led to me being able to pray with them or for them. As I reflect on that service, it was one small step to being obedient to what God was calling me to do.

I discovered that to serve it meant taking on the heart of a true servant. You may wonder what I mean by that and I am sure that this may be a very different experience for everyone. For me, it was that God taught me that to serve I had to be humble and have a humble heart. So, you ask, *'how did you learn this lesson.'* At first, I was arrogant enough to think that I really understood what it is to be humble. Little did I know that God meant business with me.

During my business career, I had been driven to always excel. I discovered that the more I gave of myself by taking on more and more responsibilities and learning new roles and acquiring new skills, I was rewarded with bigger and more important roles. Then I reached a point where I hungered for recognition and affirmation, and I yearned for being an equal to my male counterparts in similar roles. It was a hard and a difficult path to follow. I worked what felt like three, sometimes four times as hard to achieve the same recognition. This was not unusual in the business environments that I worked in and was accepted by all as a given in these male dominated companies. I worked my way through the ranks and was challenged by experiencing political jostling for positions, and seeing first hand and often being the victim too of corporate jealousy and bullying. It was not a healthy environment.

Then I faced a cultural challenge too. I was a Zambian born female in an Executive role in a Japanese organisation. How was that even possible? If you understand a little bit about cultural differences and how in some cultures, women are not deemed to be qualified enough to hold senior roles, this may make you smile. But it will also help you understand how hard I had pushed myself to achieve a role like this.

The day finally came, when God decided that I had reached my pride pinnacle. I arrived at work on that Wednesday morning and was surprised to be called into our CIO's office. He was accompanied by one of the Senior Human Resource specialists. I knew the writing was on the wall. I sat down and could feel myself tremble. Yes, you guessed it, I was informed that I was being made redundant. My role was being changed along with the roles of four of my male colleagues.

What followed was my first steps of a transition. I struggled with the mental anguish and rejection that this had created in me. I knew that God was with me in the process as I had an incredible sense of calm about me and a sense of peace throughout the weeks that followed as the corporate processes were being completed. There was one well of strength I was drawing water from and it was the ongoing prayers of my husband and fellow Christian friends and prayer warriors. They brought an immeasurable comfort during a rocky and uncertain time.

The door had finally closed on this corporate world and all that it represented. I could not identify with the huge sense of relief that I felt at first. It felt strange. Then it hit me like a ton of bricks and the anger and sense of loss set in. For a few months afterwards I wandered around feeling like I was punch drunk. I could not work out or understand why I felt so lost. It was a type of grieving process. I recognised that grief can come in many circumstances, not through a death of a person.

And then, as I was asking God why this had happened to me, I heard Him say in a still voice: *'Because my child, your identity was so wrapped up in who you had become in your corporate role, that you forgot all about who I am.'* I realised for the first time how I had been drawn in more and more, deeper, and deeper, into believing that my whole sense of who I was could only be recognised in my Job role and title. God knew that this redundancy was the first step I had to take, to recognise that my identity was not to be found in my job role and job title. Before He could finally start moulding me and making me be the person, He wants me to be, serving Him and working for His Kingdom purposes, I had to go through this fall and I fell very hard. I realised my life needs to be dedicated to following wherever He may lead and the footsteps He wants me to take to keep me on the right path, His path.

I love the way Priscilla Shirer describes and summarises where I am in one sentence in her book *He Speaks to Me, preparing to hear from God (Pg 25)* that '*our ability to hear God's voice begins when we reverence Him through simple obedience.*'[12].

This is my time to learn the lesson of obedience and to be obedient.

# 19

# Courage, Faith, and Perseverance

*'Run your race Dianne and dare to have the courage to do what God has called you to do. The race is not over yet.'* These words kept ringing in my head. *'It is time to step into your God directed purpose and time to use the voice that He has given you.'*

As I sat at my desk, my eyes fell on the verse in front of me on my pinboard. It was another of God's never-failing promises shared in John 15:7 and it says *'but if you remain in me and my words remain in you, you may ask for anything you want, and it will be granted.'* 'Is this true for me?' I wondered. How is it then that at my lowest points and in the depth of the abyss in some of my struggles, it felt at times as if I was praying but He was absent or He was not listening. God is always with us in the middle of the storms. Probably because being human, I expected an instant answer or a physical or visible sign that I could hold onto. Why is it that we often look for some visual confirmation and if we cannot see the proof immediately in some tangible form, we think that nothing is happening? I recognised that I would not be sitting here now in front of my pinboard if this promise was not true. I knew as I knew as I knew in my heart, that it was because even though I felt I was being ignored, or He was not hearing me, that God is always faithful.

I may not have had the strength to pray for myself at those times but I know how my family and some of my friends had stepped into the gap and been praying for me and interceding on my behalf. This is the amazing thing about God, that even when I was either too anxious or felt my faith was too weak for Him to lift me up, shield me and heal me, He loves me unconditionally and has protected me. He loves all His children. My friend this includes both of us and clearly, He has purpose for my life, otherwise I would not still be here. He has purpose for your life too.

God reminded me that this life that He has given me is His gift. This life I have is not about me. It is about Him and the task He has set before me which is to share His love with everyone in my world around me. He has brought me across continents, He has led me to different continents and each experience has been about helping me see more of His kingdom and learn about His kingdom people. I now know that I need to keep praying, keep moving and keep sharing my faith and tell the story of the blessings of hope and peace that a life following Him brings.

There are many stories and encounters along my journey that have proved this to me time and time again. One year, as I sat in a Colour Women's Conference, we were in a conference session focussed on one of the areas of humanitarian work that some of the proceeds from this conference was sponsoring. Are you familiar with some of the struggles and wars that rage in many countries on the African continent? As an African myself, I may be a bit closer to a little knowledge of these as sometimes only selective news from the African continent reaches the rest of the globe. I would like to share the story of one of these struggles and absolute miracles with you if you will allow me to, as women remain some of the most marginalised and wounded people in Africa.

An organisation called Watoto in Uganda founded by Gary and Marilyn Skinner, partnered with Pastor Bobbie Houston and The Colour Sisterhood in 2008. I was privileged to attend this conference in London and it was here, that I was taught a heart and gut-wrenching lesson in courage and shown hope in a physical way. Out of this conference and the joint initiative, the *Living Hope program* was started. It's focus and aim to restore dignity to women. Many teenage girls and women in Northern Uganda had come under abduction and attack from around 2003 from the rebel army in Northern Uganda, the LRA soldiers. These young women had noses, ears and lips savagely hacked off by the rebel army soldiers. It was Lillian Anena's story that totally broke my heart.

"Anena grew up in Atyak in Nwoya District, northern Uganda. On the 5 March, 2003, a rebel in the LRA (Lord's Resistance Army rebels) attacked her and cut off her left ear. She was found by a kind stranger who took her to a doctor for treatment but she was left deformed.

In 2011, the Watoto reconstructive team was sent to Anena's village after having been directed there by the doctor who first treated her. Two years later, she was taken to CORSU (Comprehensive Rehabilitation Services for Uganda) where her operation was held. "I was scared before the surgery but when they worked on me, it looks so beautiful. I am very grateful to all the people that made it possible for my ear to be recreated...I can't thank Watoto enough."[13] Hillsong Collected Blog – Colour Sisterhood Sep 14 2015]    https://www.google.com/search?client=firefox-b-d&q=colour+sisterhood+2014

We were shown a video of part of her restorative journey. The aim of the Colour Sisterhood initiative was to raise enough money to enable some of these women to have facial reconstructive surgeries (and not for vain cosmetic purposes in case the thought crosses your mind), so that they could have their faces and their smiles back and be able to break into a smile at their future again. The absolute horror of how these women were butchered and these horrendous acts of capture and war are simply too inhumane to linger over and unless I had seen the video footage and evidence of this, I think it would have been impossible to accept that one human could do this to another totally vulnerable and helpless human being.

Theirs was a journey of courage, faith, and seeing their hope fulfilled, hope for a brighter future being granted by the kindness and love of people who care and have a heart after God's own heart. Have you been able to identify with this level of caring for someone you do not know or have never met? There are so many horrendous atrocities going on around the world and we can all get to play a part in making a difference

Let me share a lesson taught by Christine Caine from Isaiah 43:19 and 2 Samuel 5:4. From Isaiah we see God is doing a new thing. Christine highlights from this verse that everything in life is a heart issue. 2 Samuel 5:4: tells of an appointing. She identifies how there is always a gap between the anointing and the appointing and there is always a season of development between the two.

Bobbie Houston could not have penned or described it better in the *Groovy Colour Diary of 2012* when she wrote these words: *'God knows what lies within us and He knows what lies before us…this is going to be a year of strengthening, refreshing and watering, so that the true potential within will mature and emerge in its fulness.'*[14]

I want to encourage you to persevere through the storms of life, look at the lighthouse to light the way and hold onto the anchor, Jesus, who is our eternal hope. I want to remind both you and I of Psalm 23 vs 1 (NIV) and of the most wonderful promise of hope: *'The Lord is my Shepherd; I shall not want'*

# 20
# Rainbows and Kisses

Come to Bermuda with me and discover the rainbow. Close your eyes for a moment. Imagine a radiant blue sky and marshmallow, fluffy white clouds scattered on the horizon. The green landscape dotted with lush palm trees and set against the hill, typical Bermudian style colonial houses. Some are larger than others but each of them oozes luxury and relaxation. The white, lacy trelliswork might be rusted in places but it does not detract from the long verandas that they all display. I realise that I am probably on the luxurious and most expensive part of the island. As I walked along the breach front, the pink sand glistened in the sunlight. I had to stoop and pick it up and let it trickle slowly through my fingers. How on earth did it end up this beautiful blush and rose-tinted pink? As far as the eye could see the entire beach was – yes, you have guessed it, pink.

This was the first time I had visited Bermuda, a true reflection of paradise on earth and I had never seen pink sand and I certainly had not heard of it before. I was so used to the African seashores painted with pure golden sands. I made a mental note to ask one of the local islanders about this interesting phenomenon and why the beaches in Bermuda are famous for this striking pink sand. Until you have seen it, you will find it hard to believe that it exists. I lingered and as I lingered it suddenly struck me how incredible God's creation is. I felt like I had felt God kiss my cheek for a moment. His creation and nature never cease to introduce new surprises if you stop and take time to open your eyes and really look at what is all around you.

'So *why does this matter?*' you may be asking. I realised years later as I considered this beautiful memory on my island visit to Bermuda, how awestruck I was by its incredible beauty and tranquillity. It is this gem in the middle of an ocean that when the hurricanes rage and the skies clear, you see the most striking rainbows adorn the skies. The storms can be quite severe and none less so, than when I was working on the island.

When the alarm was sounded that a hurricane was coming in and the winds had already started whipping up quite severely, I remember how calmly and collectively all the staff seemed to know what to do. As a visitor, I was escorted with the team I was working with and found myself in the basement of the Butterfield Bank. It was to be our place of refuge for the next few hours, possibly even couple of days and out of the way of the storm. I remember how anxious and scared I was.

As we busied ourselves with work and everyone continued with their own activities, the storm raged outside. I kept saying to myself repeatedly, *'God is with me and I know He will not let anything happen to me.'* It felt like an eternity that I kept repeating this to myself. It was the only thing that calmed the voices in my head that kept telling me that at any moment the whole building would collapse around us. How on earth had I gone from that serene and calm walk on the stunning pink beach yesterday to finding myself hidden, buried underground in a basement and I wondered what devastation might confront us when we were able to return to ground levels again.

Storms always remind me of the story shared in the Bible about when Jesus climbed into a boat on the lake with his disciples. There was the fiercest of storms, so fierce that the waves were crashing over their boat and Jesus was sleeping. His disciples were really scared and they woke Jesus telling him they were going to drown. I imagine how much worse it must have been for them because whilst I was shielded, I was relatively safe in the basement of a building. They were in a small boat on the sea and in the eye of the storm. The lesson that Jesus taught them was that they did not need to be afraid, they needed to have faith and he calmed the storm around them. (Matthew 8: 23 – 27), (Mark 4:35 - 41), (Luke 8:22 – 25). (NLT)

That evening following my walk on Horseshoe Bay Beach (it is the island's most famous pink sand beach on the south side of the island), I chatted to one of my Bermudan work colleagues and asked her how it was and why it was that the sand on the beaches was this beautiful pink colour. 'Well,' she said *'they are created by tiny grains of coral, bits of Foraminifera, which are tiny single-celled red organisms that grow beneath the coral reefs and crushed seashells mixing with soft white sand.'* How fascinating, even if a little scientific and how beautiful.

When we face our storms in life, it may certainly feel like we are being pounded and crushed by the crashing waves, into tiny bits like the coral reefs and seashells. We can make a choice to put our faith in Jesus, to be kissed on the cheek and comforted by our loving heavenly Father. Jesus is amid every storm with us if we will let Him be. All we must do is ask him to be right beside us and to reach out for His hand. He can calm the storm in your life as He has calmed many storms in my life. It does not mean that I do not still get scared or anxious or fearful as I go through each new storm that comes along. Even though the storms may not disappear, or even stop coming at us, Jesus can strengthen you through it. God is always with us even when we do not realise it and He is always ready to take your hand if you will let Him.

After each storm and when we eventually come out the other side, we will reflect those beautiful salmon pink, sandy beaches, unique, beautiful, and serene. Kissed by heaven.

Rainbow, I am sure you understand rainbows are symbolism of God's promises.

# NEW BEGINNINGS - GOD'S PROMISE

I found it no co-incidence that when Queen Elizabeth died, one of the most significant things that followed, was the appearance of the rainbows in the skies. There are probably many people that did not even notice it and if they did, may not have understood the significance that they held. There was one over Buckingham Palace, one over Balmoral Castle and one over Windsor Castle. Each of these rainbows a reminder that God loves us and is waiting for us in eternity.

# 21

# The Jewel in the Crown

There was a solemn silence and a dark sombre mood, yet it was tainted with a lightness in my spirit. The newsreader on BBC television was sombre, dressed in black and I knew the time had come of the Queen's passing. Her reign had been the longest in modern history. She was also the longest reigning Monarch of my time. Her coronation had taken place four years before I was born so she represented my understanding of what the role of a Monarch embodied. Until I stopped to reflect.

*What was the one key thing that she had represented for me?* Instantly I knew the answer without hesitation. It was her steadfast faith and her belief in Jesus Christ and our heavenly Father, God. I always knew that she was referred to as the defender of the

Christian faith in her role as sovereign of the United Kingdom. I had never stopped to ask myself whether this was fact or if it was a façade, a staged religiosity. We see so much evidence of this in our modern-day society. When the Archbishop of Canterbury paid respect to her during her funeral service, he said that she had *'served not only her nation, but also her God and King.'* I knew this to be true as she had spoken very openly of her faith in her later years.

Speaking of royalty, have you ever stopped to reflect on the crown jewels or even been to see them in the Tower of London? When we had newly returned to England after living abroad for several years, I remember my excitement at planning my first trip to the Tower of London and specifically to visit and view the crown jewels. When the actual occasion happened and I saw these sparkling crowns and gemstones, it was a breath-taking sight. There were more crowns than I had anticipated or even knew of, each with their own significance and associated history. They were encrusted with diamonds and jewels of various sizes, shapes, and dazzling colours and sizes of which I had never seen in any jewellery stores. Their brightness sparkled and dazzled behind seriously alarmed glass screens, with cameras and security visible everywhere (and probably some invisible security too).

These were the same jewels that had adorned the head of the late Queen and all the monarchs that came before her and will now adorn the head of the new King Charles III. In that moment it brought the vivid contrast to mind of this imagery and the image of the one and only crown that Jesus wore. A crown of thorns, wooden, sharp, and dull. The only glistening that would have been evident, the reflection of light in His precious blood that poured down his head from where the thorns had pierced his skull and his brow. Yet His crown was more precious than any human and jewelled crown can ever be.

God has promised us a long life if we love Him and acknowledge Him. Psalm 91 affirms this promise. His promises are true and He is constant and faithful. There has never been one promise that He has not kept or not fulfilled. And when I reflected on the life of His servant, the late Queen Elizabeth II, I know this with absolute certainty.

She loved the Lord and she was blessed with a long life here on earth and now lives in eternity. In August 2022 during one of her speeches, she made this very clear and unambiguous statement regarding where her source of strength really lay when she said: 'Throughout my life, the message and teachings of Christ have been my guide, and in them I find hope.' I know that this is real and this is what keeps me grounded. Have you met Jesus yet dear friend and do you know that there is life after death for you as there is for me?

Jesus's crown of thorns for our crown of Glory. Jesus paid for us all to be forgiven of our sins, healed, and saved. The real jewel in the crown of thorns is that Jesus wore that crown of thorns for both you and me. What a promise. My prayer is that God's Word will also be your guide and Jesus, your eternal hope just as He was Her Majesty's and is for anyone who will accept Him as their Lord and Saviour. Jesus is my eternal hope.

# 22

# The Coronation

I find it striking and poignant that the one big event that everyone around me is talking about currently, is the Coronation of King Charles III. As I am watching the preparations underway it is fascinating to see all the planning and details that are going into this next big event in English history. Suddenly there is an increase in publicity as the royal branding campaign has gained momentum and bunting and banners are making their appearance. The air is abuzz with who will attend the coronation ceremony and who has been invited to attend the Windsor music festival and where the coronation street parties are being held.

There are at least 100 world leaders that will converge on London to be part of the coronation ceremony at Westminster Abbey as everyone takes to the world stage. It is also a global event as the eyes of the world will be on the new monarch this weekend. We know the exact date, time, and place that it will take place and by the time this book is published the event will have become a historic account.

King Charles will arrive wearing King George VI's crimson robe of state. Once the service is over, he will leave Westminster Abbey wearing King George VI's purple robe of State. The Deputy Surveyor of the King's Works of Art at the Royal Collection Trust, Caroline de Guitaut, said that the robes are not only significant for their historic value but also for their sacred use during the coronation ceremony. She also said that the symbolic garments serve as a reminder of the rich history and tradition of the British monarchy. These regal garments are what the world values as symbols of what it is prepared to accept and acknowledge as important, or portraying someone of great significance and importance in our society. With all the pageantry, pomp and ceremony that will be viewed by millions across the globe, it has brought me to reflect on the parallel of The Coronation of King Jesus.

Whilst King Charles will wear a crown of gold, diamonds and precious stones, Jesus wore a crown of thorns when he was crucified at Calvary. Charles will be clothed in royal robes, that have been worn through the centuries at previous coronations. Jesus was clothed in blood-soaked cloth and when they nailed him to the cross, he was without any clothes. The robes of crimson and purple draw attention to the crimson blood-soaked loin cloth that Jesus wore. The crimson robe that will flow across King Charles's shoulders contrasts so vividly with the crimson blood that Jesus shed as his wounds bled and the blood flowed from his side where He had been pierced. King Charles's throne is an ornate and regal throne chair used for centuries during the coronation ceremonies in all the centuries past, but the throne of our Lord Jesus was the cross.

We are tied to our King Jesus by His blood that He shed on that cross at Calvary for us and that weaves us into the tapestry of the cross. Because of the sacrifice He made for us, we will not ever have to endure the suffering, torture, mocking and pain He did.

That does not mean we will not have any trials during our lifetime here on earth. We will still go through our own times of real struggle, hardship, and pain, of disappointment, loss and heartache and having to climb each mountain as it arises and experience each of the valleys. But the greatest hope we have is that we will never walk that road alone or face that challenge on our own. King Jesus goes before us, travels the path with us and covers our back to make sure we do not fall backwards.

Finally, today the Coronation service took place in Westminster Abbey. King Charles III, the 40$^{th}$ and the oldest monarch to be crowned at the Abbey. He was very pensive for most of the ceremony and even looked nervous at different stages. One such moment was when he was presented with the Bible and he asked Archbishop Justin Welby whether he should touch it. In attendance were more than one hundred heads of state and state dignitaries and two thousand three hundred guests filled the Abbey. We saw representation of all faiths take part in the service.

The striking moment happened when Archbishop Welby lifted the St. Edward's crown high in the air, before slowly lowering it onto King Charles's head and simultaneously declaring *God save the King,* before stepping back and the congregation simultaneously chanted *'God save the King.'* The abbey's bells rang out and the new monarch was declared. There were emotional moments too during the formalities of the service.

The one catching everyone's attention was seeing Prince William, the Prince of Wales, pledge allegiance to his father King Charles III. After kneeling in front of his father declaring he would be his *'liege man of life and limb,'* he arose, touched his father's crown, and then gently planted a kiss on his left cheek.

A very solemn King showed a slight hint of emotional tenderness at that point as Prince William withdrew from him. After the investiture and once the royal procession reached Buckingham Palace, we saw the thousands upon thousands of royal followers that filled Admiralty Way and the crowds that thronged to the palace gates, all to catch a glimpse of the newly crowned King once he appeared on the palace balcony.

I could not help but contrast this to the Crucifixion, when the crowds had thronged the streets of Jerusalem to witness Jesus being brutally whipped and beaten after He had been condemned to death, before carrying his cross to His crucifixion which took place at Golgotha. There was so much jeering and mocking of Him as the crowds rejected Him and yet he endured it all for us.

Jesus gave his life, a human sacrifice, for you and for me so that we can be forgiven of our sins and have hope eternal of an everlasting life.

To Jesus be all the glory, honour, and praise. Selah.

# 23

# A Royal Birth - No other but Jesus

The temperature is minus six degrees C outside and as I look out of the large windows in front of me in the conservatory, it looks like a winter wonderland in our garden. Every tree branch and wooden twig are coated in white crystals. The ground is covered in a blanket of white and it would seem as though someone has emptied a gigantic bag of powdered icing sugar all over every square inch and every blade of grass. It has been a good week. England has started experiencing the chill of the Arctic winds and weather streams from the North. There are sparrows, a redwing, a few blackbirds, and woodpigeons all pecking away at the bird seeders and gathering up the seed that has fallen on the icy ground. The blessing of seeing our regular little robin come and have a little feed from the window seeder is an extra treat today. He is a shy little fellow and I love him to bits. How on earth do these tiny little birds survive such a harsh winter?

Freeze! As the male and female blackbird are scurrying after each other I cannot help but hope that they have a warm nest to fly back to. When I take the time to sit still and simply observe all that is around me, it only takes a few moments to realise how wonderful God's creation is and how every tiny detail matters to Him.

Even while we are in this new season of winter in the Northern Hemisphere, my brother and his family will be enjoying the dawning of their summer season in the Southern Hemisphere. It is still a change and a transition. All of us are eagerly awaiting that arrival of the important Christmas celebration.

Have you found yourself getting lost in being buffered by all the advertisements, commercial drives, and parties? Perhaps you have forgotten the importance of this celebration and what it signifies? We are so overrun by the commercialisation of Christmas and the busyness of getting so much squeezed into the last few weeks of the year. I suspect that if you are anything like me, you are juggling and trying to re-prioritise so that you can get everything done in time. What do those Christmas preparations look like in your world?

It seems so urgent to take time out now, even if it is for fifteen minutes. Go and put on the kettle, make a cup of your favourite brew, and find a comfy sofa. I would like to transport us both back to the days before Christmas around two thousand and twenty-three years ago. This account of what the scene may have been is my view of how imagine their journey progressed.

Joseph and Mary were travelling from Nazareth where they were living, to Bethlehem. The reason for their journey at this stage of Mary's pregnancy was because the Roman emperor had given an order that a census needed to be recorded of all people in their hometown. The road was rough, dusty and I can imagine very dry and quite barren. The countryside was brown and the sun beat down, leaving heatwaves creating shimmers in the distance. Mary was heavily pregnant and uncomfortable now (as her transport was on the back of a donkey), as she knew her time to deliver her baby could not be too long now. When they arrived at their destination, Bethlehem, it was to be informed that there was no accommodation for them anywhere as all the travelling inns were full. Imagine the dismay that Joseph must have felt and the weariness Mary must have endured in her physical body.

One of the Innkeepers, seeing their faces, had a compassionate heart and he offered them his stable at the Inn as a place to stay. Relieved, Mary and Joseph settled in with the animals that were already sleeping amongst the hay. Yes, you guessed right. Shortly after their arrival and the tiring journey that had taken them days on the road, Mary went into labour. Then the greatest love story ever told unfolded. *'Today in the town of David a Saviour has been born to you; he is the Messiah, the Lord.'* Luke 2:11 (NIV). Mary gave birth to Jesus, a beautiful baby boy. *'.. and she gave birth to her firstborn, a son. She wrapped him in cloths and placed him in a manger, because there was no guest room available for them.'* Luke 2:7 (NIV). With no other place to lay him, he was placed in the animals' feeding trough, a manger, as his bed. '*She will give birth to a son, and you are to give him the name Jesus, because he will save his people from their sins.*' Matthew 1:21 (NIV)

If you are familiar with farming sheds or barns as we are, living where we do in the countryside, you will be familiar with the roughness and prickliness of the hay and the sounds and smells of the animals. Compared to our modern society hospital delivery rooms or comfortable homes where babies are born today, it is hard to think of how Mary must have felt. Yet her mother's heart was only focussed on her baby. Both her and Joseph totally overcome with joy and love. Their surroundings did not matter. It was Jesus that held their attention.

When an angel appeared to shepherds who were minding their flocks in fields close to Bethlehem, they were startled and very scared. However, the angel gave them reassurance and he shared with them the great story and news that Jesus, Saviour, and Messiah, had been born. This is where our living hope, Jesus, became human to live among us and teach us and show us the way for our future. This is the Royal birth that brought hope to all of us, for an eternal life and the promise that **hope reigns** eternal. What a promise.

# Conclusion

'May I ask you a question? What next for you or what is the next big event you are expectant of in your life? It could be a totally unexpected and unplanned event. Have you given this any thought?' In return, you may well be asking what my plan or strategy is. If it is like the coronation, this historic, well-orchestrated event that took to the global stage, surely there must be a plan.

Then let me summarise the **7 main steps** I have learned and referenced through this story as I have navigated conquering each mountain and walking through each of the deepest valleys in my life:

- My first step was learning the answer to **overcoming fear, which is to have faith.** It is a choice you make to believe in God's love for you. There is a great promise that confirms this for us. It is found in Isaiah 41:10: (ESV) *'Don't be afraid, for I am with you. Don't be discouraged, for I am your God. I will strengthen you and help you. I will uphold you with my victorious right hand.'* Selah. Do not let legitimate fears and insecurities hold you back. We are promised that Jesus has all bases covered even when we are faced with troubles. John 16:33: (ESV) *'I have said these things to you, that in me you may have peace. In the world you* *will have tribulation. But take heart, I have overcome the world.*' We know that we will never be left to cope on our own to find solutions or fathom things out on our own if we let Him help us and we lean into Him. Psalm 34:17-18: (ESV) '*When the righteous cry for help, the Lord hears and delivers them out of all their troubles. The Lord is near to the broken-hearted and saves the crushed in spirit.*' Selah.

- I have learned to **fix my eyes on Jesus in whom my eternal hope reigns**. I have tried to learn to do this daily and not only when that disaster, challenge, tragedy, or turmoil strikes. It is not always easy but with each new day I try again and I keep trying. Prayer and talking to Him changes everything.

- **Actively seeking direction from God** and not merely thinking that I know it all or that I have all the answers because I do not. Psalm 143:8 '*let the hear in the morning of your steadfast love, for in You I trust. Make me know the way I should go, for to you I lift up my soul.*' This includes a conscious surrender on my part.

- We may think we are in control but we really are not. **I try not to solve whatever the challenge is on my own anymore** because I have learned that I cannot do this in my own strength. It seems we always want to hand over control to Him and then somehow end up taking it back again. I am so guilty of this. The lesson I have learned is that once I have brought it to the foot of the cross, I need to let go and leave it there. Jesus is faithful and He is far more able than we can or ever will be.

- The temptation is there for us to continue in old ways and to follow what we have always done before. I have come to realise that the more you look back at the past, the more you keep harming yourself. We need **to keep looking forward and keep our hope fixed on Jesus** as He has gone before us and knows the way.

- Do you get caught in the trap of also having a victim mentality? I was challenged on this specific issue and I took away an important lesson. **We are not victims with Jesus at our side. We are victorious and the victors.** There is no room for self-pity as harsh as that may sound. He told us in John 16:33 (ESV) that we would experience trouble, '*I have said these things to you, that in me you may have peace. In the world you will have tribulation,*' but He also promised us that we will have peace because '*But take heart; I have overcome the world.*' John 16:33 (ESV) We should celebrate as we follow King Jesus because through Him, we are overcomers.

- **God's timing is always perfect.** I have challenged myself and asked why it has taken me so long to write my story. With new eyes I can see the significance and timing of what I am able to share now and I understand that God's hand is on me as He continues to give me courage and mould me. I know I had to reach a certain stage of healing and spiritual maturity first. He is always teaching us if we let Him and we continue to learn and grow, fed by Him, and fed by His Word.

Our passions often determine our direction in life. If I examine all the threads of the different passions in my life, I can see how they are all woven together. I know that through Jesus' blood over my life, I am woven into God's tapestry, just as you are.

All the mountains, valleys and life experiences are preparation for His Kingdom purpose. Now, more than ever, in this current time and place, it is time to stand up and be counted as a believer in Jesus Christ. With so much pain, strife, and anguish in the world around us, it is time to put on the full armour of God and be a *Prayer Warrior*. I have had a vision that it is time to pick up the sword of the Spirit and to be praying and praying in earnest against all the dark forces coming into lives. The enemy has created confusion, deceit, and death and comes to rob, destroy, and kill but we have a God who is more powerful. John10:10 (ESV) *'The thief comes only to steal and kill and destroy; I have come that they may have life, and have it to the full.'*

Have you got children or grandchildren? What are your concerns for them today? My biggest concern is when I recognise the world that my little granddaughters, our new generation, Gen-Z, and those future generations still to come are now a part of. There are no more shields or layers of protection. The only shield of protection is the shield of Faith and the full armour of God. Can you identify or imagine what your part is in all this chaos that is our world today and what it will continue to grow into? It is a world that is getting darker by the day.

Christine Caine, a well-known author, evangelist and founder of the A-21 anti-human trafficking movement spoke these words as she brought one of her Spirit-led messages to a close after a Sunday service at Hillsong Church in Surrey, U.K. *'There is always a season of development between the anointing and the appointing.'*[15] In one of her more recent messages, she addresses the area of building resilience and endurance (perseverance) into our lives. In it she encourages us to run our race with endurance. She describes how the word *endure* is defined as having the ability to withstand pain or hardship and to continue and keep going, despite fatigue, stress, or other adverse conditions. We have the power to face all the challenges in our lives with Jesus Christ in us, with our hope planted firmly in Jesus and not in our circumstances.

This message is real. I have heard God calling me for over 13 years to share my story, yet never understood why I could not use my voice in all this time. Now I understand. It has taken Him this time to prepare me to take up His appointment. At the start of this year, Pastor Joseph Prince shared what God had laid on his heart, that this is the year of '*Kairos*'[16], the Greek word meaning being in the right place and at the right time. As much as I have tried to drift away from it, sometimes in denial, I have discovered that it is never too late to have a voice. I know that time is now. During one of my darkest hours in Canada, God revealed this to me on paving stones at a location I was visiting on the day: '*One day you will tell your story of how you've overcome what you are going through now, and it will become part of someone else's survival guide.*'

God loves you and I know He loves me. If you have not invited Him into your life yet, it is never too late. The time is now. There is always help and there is always *Hope*. God will help you find hope after despair and brokenness. He heals the broken.

It is time now for us to have confidence in who God has created us to be, to make a difference in this world and stepping out into the broken world to do that. Know that you are believed in and that YOUR story matters in the world too. God is using His children to reach the broken, downcast, alienated and the lost.

How are you going to play your role? God wants your heart dear friend. If you do not know what your role is or maybe you think you know, but are not sure yet, perhaps now is the time to simply spend time with God and to ask Him what is next? He will lead you through the transition until you can see more clearly. He will hold your hand and walk beside you through the valleys and up to the summit. Hold on with courage and perseverance, run your race and never lose hope. As your hope rises, so your faith will rise. Your mountain is moving and this is a new day.

*'Don't fret or worry. Instead of worrying, pray. Let petitions and praises shape your worries into prayers, letting God know your concerns. Before you know it, a sense of God's wholeness, everything coming together for good, will come and settle you down. It's wonderful what happens when Christ displaces worry at the centre of your life.'* Philippians 4:6-7 (MSG).

I love Ecclesiastes 3 and want to close with this extract from it found in verses 1 – 12: (ESV)

*For everything there is a season, and a time for every matter under heaven:*

*a time to be born and a time to die, a time to plant and a time to pluck up what is planted,*

*a time to kill and a time to heal, a time to break down and a time to build up,*

*a time to weep and a time to laugh; a time to mourn and a time to dance,*

*a time to cast away stones and a time to gather stones together;*

*a time to embrace and a time to refrain from embracing;*

*a time to seek, and a time to lose; a time to keep and a time to cast away,*

*a time to tear and a time to sew; a time to keep silence and a time to speak;*

*a time to love, and a time to hate, a time for war and a time for peace.*

*What gain has the worker from his toil? I have seen the business that God has given to the children of man to be busy with.*

*He has made everything beautiful in its time. Also, He has put eternity in man's heart, yet so that he cannot find out what God has done from the beginning to the end. I perceived that there is nothing better for them than to be joyful and to do good as long as they live.'* Selah


I pray that you will find courage, hope, strength, and healing as you spend time in His presence. By God's amazing grace, you can prevail over your circumstances. Learning to see life through a lens with an eternity perspective, can change how we navigate the storms of life. We are spiritual people having a human experience and because Jesus is alive today, we have eternal life when we accept Him as our Saviour.

This is your time for release, healing, and freedom. To God be all the glory! Hebrews 12:1-3(NIV) *'let us run with perseverance the race marked out for us, fixing our eyes on Jesus, the pioneer and perfecter of faith. For the joy set before him he endured the cross, scorning its shame, and sat down at the right hand of the throne of God. Consider him who endured such opposition from sinners, so that you will not grow weary and lose heart.'*

# References

**Chapter 2**

[1] Compassion website: https://www.compassionuk.org/about-us/who-we-are/

[2] Brochure 2010 conference prepared by Pastor Bobbie Houston. Distributed publicly.

[3], [4] Just 3 Dads website: https://www.3dadswalking.uk/

[5] Just 3 Mums website: https://www.justthreemums.org.uk/

**Chapter 6**

[6] INSEAD website: https://www.insead.edu/

[7] Bobbie Houston, The Sisterhood. (Page 249) Copyright 2016 by Bobbie Houston. Published by Hodder & Stoughton, in association with Faith Words, a division of Hachette Book Group, Inc. written by permission of Hodder & Stoughton. www.hodderfaith.com. Written by permission.

**Chapter 7**

[8] Museum of the Order of St. John website: https://museumstjohn.org.uk/our-story/history-of-the-order/

## Chapter 10

[9] *https://my.clevelandclinic.org/health/diseases/24226-phyllodes-tumors* Written by The American Cancer Society medical and editorial content team, last revised June 15, 2022.

## Chapter 17

[10] Encyclopaedia Brittanica website:
https://www.britannica.com/question/What-is-Supermans-real-name

## Chapter 18

[11] Allen Arnold:
https://www.withallen.com/blog/the-enemy-of-our-creativity

[12] Priscilla Shirer, He Speaks to Me, preparing to hear from God (Pg 25). Copyright 2006 by Priscilla Shirer. Published by Moody Publishers. Written by permission.

## Chapter 19

[13] *Hillsong Collected Blog – Colour Sisterhood Sep 14 2015] https://www.google.com/search?client=firefox-b d&q=colour+ sisterhood+2014*

[14] The Groovy Colour Diary of 2012 conference handout Published by Hillsong Church, Australia

## Conclusion

[15] Christine Caine, Sunday service at Hillsong Church, Surrey campus, U.K.

[16] Pastor Joseph Prince, New Creation Church, online service January 2023.

# About the Author

Dianne Richardson, is no stranger to combatting trials at a physical, mental, emotional, and spiritual level. Her sporting background, corporate leadership roles, psychology studies, faith, and global travel, have guided her ability to identify with challenges and pressures in everyday life. Her story is not simply an anecdotal account of her journey. It is a story of receiving wholeness by growing in courage, faith, and perseverance. By receiving God's love, her mission is to make a difference in the lives of others. She is a wife, mother, grandmother, sister, friend, and author. She loves travel, history, writing, crafting, teaching, and baking.

# From the Publisher

GREAT BOOKS
ARE EVEN BETTER WHEN
THEY'RE SHARED!

Help other readers find this one:

- Post a review at your favourite online bookseller

- Post a picture on a social media account and share why you enjoyed it

- Send a note to a friend who would also love it - or better still, give them a copy.

THANKS FOR READING!